"The great gift of this book is that it has been written by someone with decades of parish and diocesan experience. Its conversational style draws the reader in and encourages effective habits among RCIA team members and parish communities. In Part One, Kapitan lays a firm foundation with an authentic vision of the RCIA, substantiated by the church's documents and liturgical texts. Chapter Four offers an impressive history of the church's major catechetical texts and the methods they have endorsed. In Part Two, he examines common errors in parish practice, yet offers practical solutions and effective catechetical preparations based upon Scripture. Throughout, he cites 'helpful resources' for every issue, including annotated bibliographies. This book should be mandatory reading for all who journey with catechumens and candidates."

— Rita A. Thiron, Executive Director, Federation of Diocesan
    Liturgical Commissions

"Eliot's genuine concern for and love of the RCIA comes through in this work. With its blend of personal witness, teachings of the church, and very practical suggestions and models, this text would benefit any parish's initiation ministry. You will come away from it not only with the inspiration to want to do better for those who participate in the RCIA, but also equipped to do so. Thank you for this wonderful gift!"

— Matthew Miller
    Director, Office of Worship
    Diocese of Evansville

"Eliot Kapitan's considerable experience, knowledge—and love—of the RCIA come to bear in *Unfolding the Mystery of Christ*. The vision he presents is at once faithful to the church's mission of forming disciples of Jesus Christ and a challenge to delve more deeply into the catechetical process. I am especially grateful for the practical strategies he offers and I look forward to using this book to inspire catechists in my diocese!"

— Jonathan F. Sullivan
  Director of Parish Ministries, Services, and Catechesis
  Diocese of Lafayette-in-Indiana

"Informational. Inspirational. Practical. Eliot is so knowledgeable about all aspects of the RCIA and explains formation in a way that can be understood and appreciated by the novice to the seasoned catechist. This is a resource that I will return to again and again. All will want this book in their library."

— Sue A. Huett
  Director, Department of Pastoral Services and Office of Worship
  Diocese of Belleville

Unfolding the Mystery of Christ

Sunday by Sunday Formation of Catechumens

Eliot Kapitan

LITURGICAL PRESS
Collegeville, Minnesota

www.litpress.org

1   2   3   4   5   6   7   8   9

Library of Congress Cataloging-in-Publication Data

Names: Kapitan, Eliot, author.
Title: Unfolding the mystery of Christ : Sunday by Sunday formation of catechumens / Eliot Kapitan.
Description: Collegeville, Minnesota : Liturgical Press, 2020. | Includes bibliographical references. | Summary: "A resource giving readers and RCIA teams an ordered method for preparing the Period of the Catechumenate using the Sundays of the liturgical year as the basis of the formation plan for catechumens and candidates"— Provided by publisher.
Identifiers: LCCN 2019041950 (print) | LCCN 2019041951 (ebook) | ISBN 9780814665558 (paperback) | ISBN 9780814665800 (epub) | ISBN 9780814665800 (mobi) | ISBN 9780814665800 (pdf)
Subjects: LCSH: Catholic Church. Ordo initiationis Christianae adultorum. | Initiation rites—Religious aspects—Catholic Church—Study and teaching. | Catechetics— Catholic Church—Study and teaching. | Catechists—Handbooks, manuals, etc.
Classification: LCC BX2045 .I553 K37 2020 (print) | LCC BX2045 .I553 (ebook) | DDC 268/.82—dc23
LC record available at https://lccn.loc.gov/2019041950
LC ebook record available at https://lccn.loc.gov/2019041951

Vatican II, Constitution on the Sacred Liturgy, 102
In the course of the year, moreover,
[the church] unfolds the whole mystery of Christ
from the incarnation and nativity to the ascension,
to Pentecost
and the expectation of the blessed hope of the coming of the Lord.

**Universal Norms on the Liturgical Year
and the General Roman Calendar,** 1
Holy Church celebrates the saving work of Christ
on prescribed days in the course of the year with sacred remembrance.
Each week, on the day called the Lord's Day,
she commemorates the Resurrection of the Lord,
which she also celebrates once a year in the great Paschal Solemnity,
together with his blessed Passion.
In fact, throughout the course of the year
the Church unfolds the entire mystery of Christ . . .

Rite of Christian Initiation of Adults, 1
The rite of Christian initiation presented here
is designed for adults [including children of catechetical age]
who, after hearing the mystery of Christ proclaimed,
consciously and freely seek the living God
and enter the way of faith and conversion
as the Holy Spirit opens their hearts.

Rite of Christian Initiation of Adults, 75
The catechumenate is an extended period
during which the candidates
are given suitable pastoral formation and guidance,
aimed at training them in the Christian life.

Contents

Acknowledgments

With Thanks

. . . to Sue Huett (Diocese of Belleville), Matt Miller (Diocese of Evansville), and Todd Williamson (Archdiocese of Chicago), who dreamed of ways to unfold the mystery of Christ;

. . . to my colleagues in the Federation of Diocesan Liturgical Commissions, Region VII, who collaborated on projects and prayers to foster the presence of Christ in liturgy and life;

. . . to the many team members and participants of the North American Forum on the Catechumenate who fostered a rich and compelling grasp of Christian initiation;

. . . to catechumens and candidates, their sponsors and godparents, and the faithful of countless parishes who embraced the paschal mystery;

. . . and to Jackie Kapitan, whose support and prayer helped to make this book possible.

Formation Begins with Sunday

The church has a measured way for unfolding the mystery of Christ. It occurs over time by teaching, community life, prayer, and service. It begins early in the Christian home. It continues through the school years. It is enriched in adulthood, in every age, Sunday after Sunday, until we see God face-to-face in death.

Constitution on the Sacred Liturgy

In the course of the year, moreover, [the church] unfolds the whole mystery of Christ from the incarnation and nativity to the ascension, to Pentecost and the expectation of the blessed hope of the coming of the Lord. (102)

Universal Norms on the Liturgical Year and the General Roman Calendar

Holy Church celebrates the saving work of Christ on prescribed days in the course of the year with sacred remembrance. Each week, on the day called the Lord's Day, she commemorates the Resurrection of the Lord, which she also celebrates once a year in the great Paschal Solemnity, together with his blessed Passion. In fact, throughout the course of the year the Church unfolds the entire mystery of Christ and observes the birthdays of the Saints. (1)

Because this is the long-cherished method for the faithful in Christ, by means of a weekly encounter with the fullness of Christ, the church also requires this same plan for the formation and training of catechumens, those seeking to live the Christian life in more complete ways with the grace of the initiation sacraments of baptism, confirmation, and Eucharist.

In many places, this thorough plan has collapsed by varying degrees to one of less intensity, shorter time, fewer catechists, more information delivery than anything else, and less involvement with the faithful of the parish and the diocese.

For those who have worked in this initiation ministry for a time, who has not heard the following?

Seekers Who Say:

- I do not want to/cannot spend a long time at this.
- This has to be done before the wedding.
- It will please my (future) in-laws.
- I don't want to do anything in public.

Team Members Who Say:

- I will work at this from fall to spring, but not in the summer. I need some down time.
- I will come to the sessions when I can, but additional monthly team meetings are not possible.
- I will not/cannot go to workshops or ministry training sessions, either here in the parish or in the region.
- I do not have the RCIA book. I really do not need my own copy of the ritual text. I have not opened the book.
- It is important to keep everyone together, doing the same things at the same time.
- For those who miss a session, we have to provide make-up classes so they can stay on schedule.

- We have this small group of sponsors to use over and over because they know what to do.

- Our team of ten is now only one or two. I am/we are doing the best I/we can.

Pastors and Staff Members Who Say:

- I have a lot of other things to do. I have to be more efficient with this one ministry among many others.

- I know how to do this with a sixteen- or twenty-week teaching plan that has been used over and over. I know it works. It gives them what they need.

- We can catch up on missed classes during Lent even after the Rite of Election.

- Because lay parishioners do not have a thorough academic training, I will do all or most of the teaching.

- You, Deacon, because of your academic formation and degree, have everything you need to be in charge of the RCIA. You do not need additional formation. You do not need a big team.

- The church only gives us an ideal. It is okay if we do not achieve it.

- The diocese only makes this work more difficult.

As an active participant in parish, diocesan, and regional work with Christian initiation and all of liturgy, I have heard all these complaints and expectations—and more as well.

These concerns are further complicated by some trends. Over the past twenty years or so, money is tighter, full-time catechumenal ministers on parish and diocesan staffs have been given added duties or reduced to part-time or volunteer status, diocesan and regional training is less frequent or ceased altogether, and adult learning methods and suitable catechetical methods are not always a regular part of diocesan formation curricula.

Ministers feel these pressures. Regrettably, however, giving into these pressures ultimately leads to not trusting the church. Not trusting the church's method. Not trusting the church's agenda. Not trusting the church's honored practice of reading the Bible and tradition by means of the *Lectionary for Mass*. Not trusting the biblically based way of praying. Not trusting Sunday and the liturgical year.

Additionally, these behaviors lead to trends that are of great concern.

1. A period of the catechumenate that is so short—far less than the minimum one full liturgical year—that the necessary norms for formation laid out in the *Rite of Christian Initiation of Adults* (RCIA) 75–105 (Canada, 75–104) cannot be fully addressed.

2. This closely held ministry approach of only a few people neglects the baptismal duty of all the faithful to engage in discipleship formation (RCIA 4, 9).

3. This hurried attempt at formation has ministers and parishes abandon the ancient method of formation, Sunday by Sunday, with the treasured resources of what are now the Lectionary and Missal and ritual music and the church's tradition.

4. This collapsed attempt at formation asserts that we know how to do this; my method is better; the church gives us an ideal toward which we strive (and probably not achieve) but not a mandate or duty.

But the truth is this: The church's tradition and ritual book provide a norm and not a mere ideal. They present a standard and a vision to which parish and diocesan ministers must attend. It is their duty—a duty that respects the right of seekers and catechumens to the suitable formation in the Christian life desired by the church. The norm for initiation is achievable. It is possible with time, attention, and resources.

Too much is at stake. We must regularly remind ourselves of the Christian initiation vision. Although information about Christ and

Christianity is important, formation as a Christian and conformation to Christ are central.

Aidan Kavanagh, *The Shape of Baptism: The Rite of Christian Initiation*

A *norm* . . . has nothing to do with the number of times a thing is done, but it has everything to do with the standard according to which a thing is done . . . To the extent possible, the norm must always be achieved to some extent lest it slip imperceptibly into the status of a mere "ideal" all wish for but are under no obligation to realize. (Collegeville, MN: Liturgical Press, 1991, p. 108)

The *Code of Canon Law* defines the length of a year in the section on computation of time. It is 365 days. The norm "accommodated to the liturgical year and solidly supported by celebrations of the word" (RCIA 75) is thus 365 days, 52 weeks. It is not just a liturgical season or two. It is not just an academic or school year.

Code of Canon Law

In law, a day is understood as a period consisting of 24 continuous hours and begins at midnight unless other provision is expressly made; a week is a period of 7 days; a month is a period of 30 days, and a year is a period of 365 days unless a month and a year are said to be taken as they are in the calendar. (can. 202 §1)

This, plus the fourteen-year pastoral experience with Christian initiation, led the bishops for the United States to affirm this norm in their 1986 National Statutes for the Catechumenate (which is binding for all US dioceses; see the accompanying box). The Apostolic See confirmed the statutes as conference law in 1988. The law is this: the minimum span of time for the period of the catechumenate is a whole year, reaffirming that formation is accommodated to the liturgical year specified in RCIA 75. All these statutes are found in Appendix III of the US edition. There may be rare exceptions for a shorter formation plan but only as a request to the diocesan bishop, who may grant it for cause, on a case-by-case basis (see RCIA 331; Canada, 307).

Note in this norm the use of the word "minimum." The necessary discernment concerning conversion to Christ, that is, falling in love with him who loved us first, may take *more* time (see RCIA 76). It usually does.

Rite of Christian Initiation of Adults, **Appendix III (US) National Statutes for the Catechumenate**

The period of the catechumenate, beginning at acceptance into the order of catechumens and including both the catechumenate proper and the period of purification and enlightenment after election or enrollment of names, should extend for at least one year of formation, instruction, and probation. Ordinarily this period should go from at least the Easter season of one year until the next; preferably it should begin before Lent in one year and extend until Easter of the following year. (6)

Rite of Christian Initiation of Adults

Exceptional circumstances may arise in which the local bishop, in individual cases, can allow the use of a form of Christian initiation that is simpler than the usual, complete rite (see 34.4). (331; Canada, 307)

Two Parts of This Book

In part I of this book, "Forming the Faithful in Christ," I lay out the normative way the church forms the faithful. I then make the case that since this is the way we, the baptized, are shaped into Christ, it is the suitable way for forming catechumens seeking baptism, confirmation, and Eucharist.

This is hard work. This is important work. Attempts at suitable adaptation of a rite, sometimes, can lead us to stray too far from norms intrinsic to Roman Catholic liturgy. To make it easier to review key texts, citations from related primary sources are printed in boxes within the text to connect the reader to key values, central beliefs, and required norms.

Part II, "Steps for Preparing a Week during the Period of the Catechumenate," presents an ordered method for preparing the period of the catechumenate week by week, season by season, liturgical year by liturgical year with recommended resources. Although there are books available with ready-to-use session plans (not all of which are of equal value), they should not be the starting point much less the only sources for this ministry.

Part I.
Forming the Faithful in Christ

With the advent of the reformed English editions of *Christian Initiation*, General Introduction (CIGI), in 1969 and 1973, *Rite of Christian Initiation of Adults* (RCIA) in 1974 and 1985 (with adaptations for the United States in 1988 and for Canada in 1987), and *Rite of Baptism for Children* (RBC) in 1970, it was not uncommon for church members to assume that the fourfold training and formation of catechumens—suitable catechesis, community life, prayer and liturgy, and living the apostolic life (see RCIA 75)—were either totally new or recovered from ancient ways of doing catechumenal formation.

The church, however, has always embraced these methods, even when not explicitly named. In any apprenticeship process, both within and outside church life, new members are formed in the fundamentals by those members already involved in the effort. These members teach and form by what they believe and know and practice.

In part I, therefore, we will review the ancient and traditional ways the baptized, the faithful in Christ, have been and still are shaped and formed in ongoing ways. We will also look at practical connections between this ancient pattern of formation and the *Rite of Christian Initiation of Adults*.

Chapter 1

From the Very Beginning

Story: Becoming a Grocer

My father was a grocer in a small town in South Dakota. All the children worked in the store. I started with the simple tasks of taking out the trash and sweeping the floor after school. Later, I learned to bag and carry out, first by helping one who knew how to do it. Over time, I came to know who wanted boxes or sacks, how heavy or light to pack, and how to load the car.

I learned to stock, rotate, and facedown jars and cans by watching and working with my dad in the first aisle. This included efficient organization of my part of the back room. I learned to prepare and care for produce by the coaching of my older brother. Dutch taught me how to slice meat and wrap packages. I learned to wait on trade first at the cash register and then on the telephone.

This did not happen all at once. It occurred over time, years, in fact.

Becoming a Christian

The Acts of the Apostles describes the early experience of the church. After Peter's Pentecost preaching results in the baptism of three thousand into Christ, chapter 2 concludes with a description of the common life:

> They devoted themselves
> to the teaching of the apostles and to the communal life,
> to the breaking of the bread and to the prayers . . .
> All who believed were together and had all things in common;
> they would sell their property and possessions
> and divide them among all according to each one's need.

Acts of the Apostles 2:42-47

They devoted themselves to the teaching of the apostles and to the communal life, to the breaking of the bread and to the prayers. Awe came upon everyone, and many wonders and signs were done through the apostles. All who believed were together and had all things in common; they would sell their property and possessions and divide them among all according to each one's need. Every day they devoted themselves to meeting together in the temple area and to breaking bread in their homes. They ate their meals with exultation and sincerity of heart, praising God and enjoying favor with all the people. And every day the Lord added to their number those who were being saved.

It is telling that we hear this proclamation on the Second Sunday of Easter in Year A. In some places, we may hear it every Easter season since the Year A set of Sunday readings may be used whenever the period of postbaptismal catechesis or mystagogy is celebrated, even outside the usual times (RCIA 247; Canada, 237).

We also may hear this description of the common Christian life in these celebrations:

- Ritual Masses for the Institution of Acolytes (*Lectionary for Mass*, 786)

- For the Blessing of Abbots and Abbesses (LM 807)

- For the Consecration of Virgins and Religious Profession (LM 812)

- For the Dedication or Blessing of a Church or an Altar (LM 818)

- Masses for Various Needs and Occasions, For the Holy Church (LM 828)

- For Religious (LM 853)

- Votive Mass for the Most Holy Eucharist (LM 977)

These occasions have common threads. They are gatherings of the church to pray for persons who act for the benefit of the church, for members of the church, and for the whole church and the repeatable sacrament of the Eucharist.

When we listen to this Scripture today, we uncover a pattern of formation. It is a pattern established from the very beginning of Christian life. All who believe are shaped by four things:

1. the teaching of the apostles;

2. the common life;

3. the breaking of the bread and the prayers, that is, Eucharist and daily praying;

4. and being together and sharing according to each one's needs.

All who believe struggled together to be holy. In so doing, they looked like Christ, they behaved like Christ, they became like Christ.

For the first three centuries of the church, in places where following this way was illegal, house-based ministry played an essential role in church life. It modeled Jesus's own ministry with apostles and disciples. Formation took place in secret sometimes, in public at other times. This teaching, however, was not done with chalk boards, handouts, or manuals. It was done person-to-person, often within the small group. It was done with believers sharing with seekers. It was done by sharing faith and witnessing faith, even unto death. It was done with careful discernment to test faithfulness to this Christ-based life of both seekers and practitioners. It was done as the faithful way of living in the world.

The New Testament is replete with stories of house churches. Read of the house churches of Mary, Lydia, Prisca and Aquila, Nympha, and Philemon (Acts 12:12; 16:40; Rom 16:3-5; Col 4:15; Phil 1-2). Read the lives of the early martyrs.

These examples stress that changed lives "win" new converts. These examples care less about information delivery and more about transformation of life by formation and conformation to the dead and risen Christ. The apostolic and early church stressed life over curriculum. Ministry leaned into the spiritual gifts and baptismal charisms for the good of all. Everyone was involved in some suitable way.

They took to heart and to action the words of Jesus we recall in every Mass: "Do this in memory of me." Not only did it entail the breaking of the bread and the eating and drinking at the table of the Lord, but it also included breaking open the word, breaking open lives, and pouring them out in apostolic works.

From the very beginning, Christians did this with devotion, with rapt attention, with constancy. They did it, not alone, but together. It lasted over centuries, not always in exactly the same ways but always with the same intention of faithfulness to Jesus Christ. We do this still. Sunday by Sunday. Week by week.

Practical Tips

In *Gaudete et Exsultate*, Pope Francis reminds us of our call to holiness in today's world. This is our path—holiness. Do not be afraid of it, he tells us. Attend to Christ and his church, he tells us. "Rejoice and be glad," he reminds us. This is in harmony with "The Universal Call to Holiness" taught some fifty years earlier by the Second Vatican Council (see *Lumen Gentium*, Dogmatic Constitution on the Church, 39–42). It would be helpful to read both side by side.

We can become more like Christ by attending to the fourfold method outlined in the Acts of the Apostles. Behavior is key. Here are some examples, suggestions, and practical tips.

Vatican Council II, Dogmatic Constitution on the Church

It is therefore quite clear that all Christians in whatever state or walk of life are called to the fullness of christian life and to the perfection of charity, and this holiness is conducive to a more human way of living in society here on earth. In order to reach this perfection the faithful should use the strength dealt out to them by Christ's gift, so that, following in his footsteps and conformed to his image, doing the will of God in everything, they may wholeheartedly devote themselves to the glory of God and to the service of their neighbor. (40)

Be Holy at Home

Look for times and ways in daily life to be conscious that Christ is present and living among us.

Catechism of the Catholic Church

The Christian home is the place where children receive the first proclamation of the faith. For this reason the family home is rightly called "the domestic church," a community of grace and prayer, a school of human virtue and of Christian charity. (1666)

When our son was little, we looked for ways to be Christian at home in addition to daily prayer at table and bedside. For example, we used the Advent wreath, the Christmas crèche, a box for money and household items for those in need. When away from home, we walked the church building (sometimes *during* Mass with this restless child) and told the stories in the windows and statues and poor boxes. We hung around with other families with small children and similar beliefs.

We could be holy at home, but we also knew we could not be holy alone.

Be Part of Small Groups

Trust the house church experience of the early days. Look for smaller groups, even for the short term, in which to share the faith experience. Faith life is enriched there in ways that cannot happen in the large group setting. Both are needed; both are important.

My own life is filled with participation in many small groups for prayer, study, faith sharing, and support. During my first church job, the Second Sunday gathering was a diverse group of single and married people—a college student, high school teacher, Goodwill executive, parish director of religious education, retreat giver, and retired priest.

During my first parish job, the staff began each day with coffee and conversation, followed by prayer in various forms, and lunch. There was also corporate homily prep on Tuesday and a staff meeting on Thursday.

Later, the theology study group met once a month to pore over a chosen book to sharpen our grasp of belief and faith for more effective diocesan ministry.

Later, my wife and I met for two years with four couples and one single woman for prayer, conversation, and mutual support.

Later, I poured myself into my parish catechumenal ministry as one of thirteen volunteers. In addition to grappling with the vision and tasks for initiation in a year-round format, it helped me to fall in love with weekly attention to Sunday's readings and prayers in richer ways than any previous parish or diocesan ministry.

Later, the members of the "beloved department," in my final years of diocesan ministry, enriched my life—and all of us—with monthly meetings for prayer with faith and life sharing, corporate study, and common work on overlapping concerns. This spilled over into hallway conversations, smaller interoffice projects, and collaborative efforts of greater intensity that would not have been possible without the fruits of the monthly gatherings.

The learning: no one group lasted throughout my entire life. The various groups came and went because of attending to need and grace and being the right people at the right time. Look for these vital aspects: prayer, accompaniment, presence, and collaboration. Look for people who hunger to live the Christian life in fuller ways—even imperfect people, which we all surely are—in imperfect ways.

Be Active in Adult Formation

Neither confirmation nor graduation ends our Christian formation. Look for gatherings in the parish or region or online to foster thinking, pondering, and growing in faith. Do not be afraid to read something spiritual or theological. I have a friend who stops reading novels in Advent and in Lent to give over more time to foster her faith life.

Our parish-based Growing in Faith Together (GIFT) program plunged parishioners into wrestling with the paschal mystery during a weekend retreat. In monthly gatherings of those who took part in a weekend, members were fed with prayer, discussion, food (of course), and all manner of conversation before and after the end and start time. This extended into other activity, both on and off the parish campus.

Be Charitable and Just

We cannot be Christian without doing for others in ways suited to our abilities and responsibilities. We can surely give to the various civil and church collections for special needs, but we can also look for simple and complex ways to put our hands and feet to mercy works.

I shoveled my elderly neighbor's sidewalk without asking. I would tell her when she would gently chide me, not only am I (still) healthy enough to do it, but also it recalls with gratitude the one who did it for my mother in a faraway town.

Our parish regularly gathers goods for the local food pantry, cooks for the Bread Line, delivers for Meals on Wheels, participates in Habitat for Humanity builds, and opens the Parish Center for non-parish charity efforts.

Chapter 25 of Matthew's gospel tells us the story of the Judgment of the Nations, the great divide of the sheep and the goats. It began then and continues today our necessary concern for doing works of mercy. Here is the list expanded by the US bishops and by Pope Francis.

Corporal Works of Mercy
- Feed the hungry
- Give drink to the thirsty
- Shelter the homeless
- Clothe the naked
- Visit the sick
- Visit the prisoner
- Bury the dead
- Give alms to the poor
- Care for our common home

Spiritual Works of Mercy
- Counsel the doubtful
- Instruct the ignorant
- Admonish the sinner
- Comfort the sorrowful
- Forgive injuries

- Bear wrongs patiently

- Pray for the living and the dead

- Care for our common home

Helpful Resources

Give Us This Day: Daily Prayer for Today's Catholic. Collegeville, MN: Liturgical Press, twelve issues annually.

> Contains Mass readings, prayers, and reflection for each day plus a simple setting for Morning and Evening Prayer; the Order of Mass; brief articles; suitable songs and various religious art.

Pope Francis. Apostolic Exhortation *Gaudete et Exsultate*: On the Call to Holiness in Today's World. March 19, 2018.

> Pope Francis invites us to "rejoice and be glad," reminding us of our Christian call to holiness, the most attractive face of the church. He invites us to look for the saint next door, helps us to reflect on the words of Jesus in the Beatitudes and Matthew 25 as ways to shape holy lives, and cites specific ways to be holy in today's world.

Anything that will foster small group prayer, faith sharing, conversation, and transformation. Resources with faith life discussion questions are especially helpful.

Chapter 2

Liturgy and Paschal Mystery

Story: Being United in Married Life

After forty years of marriage, I know I am still learning how marriage works. Ask my wife. I am not throwing her under the bus—we believe it is true for both of us. In fact, soon after the wedding, we pledged to work as intensely as we could at this marriage for the first fifty years—and then, based on the total experience, decide if we could reup for another fifty. We are confident we will.

We are still learning to not be lazy, to talk things out, to work on this together. We know marriage is hard work. It is done with love and affection, for sure, but also with attention, persistence, and trust. I know we know more about marriage now than we did at the wedding forty years ago. And yet, if truth be told, learning is not done. The relationship is not over.

Being United in Christ

Just as spouses are constantly learning to be married, the church is constantly learning how to be more in union with Christ. We even use marriage language to describe the relationship of Christ, the groom, with his bride, the church.

In 1962, in deciding that the church needed renewal, Pope John XXIII and the bishops of the world met in ecumenical council. It lasted four years. We still are living in these reforming ways that call us to active participation, baptismal holiness, ecumenical and interfaith endeavors, and participation in the world for the sake of the kingdom of God. Rereading, or reading for the first time, the documents of the Second Vatican Council—especially the four constitutions on the church, divine revelation, liturgy, and the church in the modern world—help us to discern if we still are on right paths and if we need any course correction.

The first document from the Second Vatican Council was the Constitution on the Sacred Liturgy (CSL) *Sacrosanctum Concilium*. It was issued on December 4, 1963, at the end of the second session devoted to prayer, study, and debate.

The council agreed, almost unanimously, that reforming the liturgy could achieve these broader conciliar goals for the good of the whole church (CSL 1):

- increasing vigor to the Christian life,

- adapting what can be adapted to the needs of our times,

- fostering unity among all believers in Christ, and

- helping to call persons into the household of the church.

Liturgy helps us to do all this. It is in this communal public prayer that the faithful in Christ celebrate whose we are and how we come to know what we believe and how we are to behave. Liturgy is, in fact, the first school of the church. It is there we hear Christ speak to us, not only long ago but today. It is there we offer eucharistic thanks and praise. It is there we are fed by him. It is there we are charged and sent to do mercy and serve the people of this age.

Vatican II, Constitution on the Sacred Liturgy

The sacred council has set out to impart an ever-increasing vigor to the Christian lives of the faithful; to adapt more closely to the needs of our age those institutions which are subject to change; to encourage whatever can promote the union of all who believe in Christ; to strengthen whatever serves to call all of humanity into the church's fold. Accordingly it sees particularly cogent reasons for undertaking the reform and promotion of the liturgy. (1)

The central mystery of our Christian belief is the triune nature of God (see *Catechism of the Catholic Church*, 234 and 261, and *United States Catholic Catechism for Adults*, chapter 5). Liturgy teaches this same truth. We begin almost every prayer "in the name of the Father, and of the Son, and of the Holy Spirit." We know it and hold it dear because of our grasp of God's great love for us and of the presence of God made human with us. This saving activity of Christ's suffering, dying, rising, and ascending is his redeeming work. Every liturgy, every public prayer of the church connects us to it. "Paschal mystery" is the shorthand for this immense reality.

Vatican II, Constitution on the Sacred Liturgy

God who "wills that all be saved and come to the knowledge of the truth" (1 Tim 2:4), "who in many times and various ways spoke of old to our ancestors through the prophets" (Heb 1:1), when the fullness of time had come, sent his Son, the Word made flesh, anointed by the Holy Spirit, to preach the Gospel to the poor, to soothe the broken hearted (see Is 61:1; Lk 4:18), to be a bodily and spiritual physician/ the mediator between God and humanity (see 1 Tim 2:5). For his humanity united with the person of the Word was the instrument of our salvation. Therefore, in Christ "our reconciliation was perfectly achieved and the fullness of divine worship was given to us." . . .

> This work of human redemption and perfect glorification of God, foreshadowed by the wonders which God performed among the people of the Old Testament, Christ the Lord completed principally in the paschal mystery of his blessed passion, resurrection from the dead, and glorious ascension, whereby "dying, he destroyed our death and rising, restored our life." . . . For it was from the side of Christ as he slept the sleep of death upon the cross that there came forth the wondrous sacrament of the whole church. (5)

Why is the paschal mystery so important and so central to our faith? How does the action of the dead and risen Christ raise us up in big and small ways? In looking at our life with eyes of faith, each of us can highlight examples that bear out this truth.

A big personal example. On my way to work one day, my car was hit from behind while stopped at a red light. We all walked away. Five weeks later, with a severe headache and a dragging left foot, I visited my doctor. She scheduled an MRI for the following day. After the reading, the neurosurgeon explained, "You have a slow bleed that is putting pressure on the brain; you need surgery right now." My wife was confident I would be okay. We both were surprisingly confident God wasn't done with me yet. That was our prayer. After five new holes in my head (friends and family didn't think I needed any more), a titanium plate, and slow healing, I recovered, but with a whole new take on life. I could have died. But I was given renewed life. Now, some things are really important; many more are less consequential.

Our lives are also filled with some small examples of living paschal mystery. Letting someone with two items go ahead of my basket full of groceries at the checkout line. Taking a coffee break with a cantankerous coworker to talk about nonwork things. Taking the last piece of cherry pie at the parish social to one who likes it as much as me. Listening to the same story told in the same way because the same person, not seeking advice, still needs to tell it one more time.

Vatican II, Constitution on the Sacred Liturgy

For the liturgy, through which "the work of our redemption takes place," . . . especially in the divine sacrifice of the Eucharist, is supremely effective in enabling the faithful to express in their lives and portray to others the mystery of Christ and the real nature of the true church. (2)

This paschal mystery is at the heart of every liturgy. To be clear on this, each ritual book of the Roman Catholic Church, in the opening paragraphs of the introduction, lays out how the sacrament or ritual activity celebrates this mystery and incorporates us into it. Note the example from the *Rite of Christian Initiation of Adults*:

> The rite of Christian initiation presented here is designed for adults who, after hearing the mystery of Christ proclaimed, consciously and freely seek the living God and enter the way of faith and conversion as the Holy Spirit opens their hearts. By God's help they will be strengthened spiritually during their preparation and at the proper time will receive the sacraments fruitfully. (1)

> The whole initiation must bear a markedly paschal character, since the initiation of Christians is the first sacramental sharing in Christ's dying and rising. (8)

Liturgy, the public prayer of the church, is the best thing we do. It is there, we know without a doubt, that the dead and risen Christ is present and living among us. We live with him and in him—and he in us.

Yet every Mass, every liturgy is not an end in and of itself. We are dismissed to "Go in peace, glorifying the Lord by your life." We are sent off the parish campus to be what we celebrate and to do what is our duty.

> ## Vatican II, Pastoral Constitution on the Church in the Modern World
>
> Mindful of the words of the Lord: "By this all will know that you are my disciples, if you have love for one another" (Jn 13:35), Christians can yearn for nothing more ardently than to serve the people of this age successfully with increasing generosity. Holding loyally to the Gospel, enriched by its resources, and joining forces with all who love and practice justice, they have shouldered a weighty task here on earth and they must render an account of it to him who will judge all people on the last day. (93)

The final document of the Second Vatican Council, issued at its close in 1965, the Pastoral Constitution on the Church in the Modern World *Gaudium et Spes*, makes this clear. The bishops declared in the closing paragraph that "Christians can yearn for nothing more ardently than to serve the people of this age successfully with increasing generosity" (93).

Clearly, the bishops did not change their minds in two years. Because liturgy is central to the Christian life, because we let ourselves be shaped by Christ and shaped into him, we cannot help but to behave like him. At every Mass, for example, we listen to Christ, give thanks to God, feed on Christ in Body and Blood, and are dismissed to love and to serve. We repeat it the following Sunday, and the next.

Liturgy builds up the church, those who belong to Christ. The church builds up the world, everyone who belongs to God. The next chapter lays out in clearer ways how, in the liturgical year, the mystery of Christ is revealed.

Practical Tips

Prayer is essential for each of us and all of us. Personal prayer is necessary. Because we believe that we are saved as a people, however, individual praying is not enough for Christians. We know this because we are rooted in the chosen people of the Old Testament—the people of Abraham and Sarah, Moses and Miriam, the Judges and the Prophets. These are our ancestors in faith. Sacrifice and prayer were always done by the people for the people. The same is true for us.

Participate in Each Sunday

This is the day, above all others, we keep holy. At the heart of it is the Liturgy of the Word and the Liturgy of the Eucharist, surely. But what else can we do in the remaining hours engendered by that celebration? Traditionally, the whole parish regathering to sing Evening Prayer is still "on the books" though it is rarely done in most places. Here are some possible adaptations for a richer focus on Christ and his glorious saving mystery on the first day of the week:

- The family can fill the afternoon with age-appropriate projects or short trips.

- Our parish, encouraged by a diocesan-wide effort, fostered monthly whole-community catechesis at 5:00 p.m., with combinations of whole group time, age group time, family time, and prayer. The event ended with dinner.

- My wife and I meet with a group that varies from four to twelve people for a late breakfast after Mass. Parish, family, city and world news, and various needs for prayer and outreach fill our conversations.

Pay Attention

It is easy, with each succeeding year, to let ourselves be distracted. Our liturgy is filled with words and music and some moments of silence—too many to savor, too many to remember. By reviewing the texts of the Lectionary and the Missal before Sunday Mass begins, I find I have a better chance to stay attuned to this communal praying. I also have a better chance to then carry an idea, a phrase, a musical refrain, or a task from the church into the week.

Vatican II, Constitution on the Sacred Liturgy

The Christian people's devotions . . . are to be highly recommended . . . But such devotions should be so drawn up that they harmonize with the liturgical seasons, accord with the sacred liturgy, are in some way derived from it, and lead the people to it, since in fact the liturgy by its very nature is far superior to any of them. (13)

Devotion Tied to Liturgy

Catholics have a rich treasury of devotional prayer, for example, the rosary, stations of the cross, novenas short and long, and a myriad of individual prayers and methods for praying. They are helpful. But they cannot be an end in themselves. They must lead to communal prayer and be in harmony with the liturgical prayer held dear by the church. If they do not, then something is amiss.

Helpful Resources

Vatican Council II: Constitutions, Decrees, Declarations; The Basic Sixteen Documents. Austin Flannery, OP, general editor. Collegeville, MN: Liturgical Press, 2014.

> This is a "readable" edition with inclusive language. The documents are also available on the Vatican website in many languages. Each household should have a copy.

United States Catholic Catechism for Adults. Washington, DC: United States Conference of Catholic Bishops, 2006. ccc.usccb.org/flipbooks/uscca/files /assets/basic-html/page-1.html.

> See chapter 14, "The Celebration of the Paschal Mystery of Christ."

Chapter 3

Sunday and the Liturgical Year

Story: Unfolding Grandma Kappy's Quilt

As children, we always treasured Grandma Kappy's visits. She loved to cook and made dishes that were not a regular part of our family meals. There was even dessert made from the produce in our yard: cinnamon apples, rhubarb crumble, and gooseberry pie.

When not in the kitchen, we would see her busy hands mending clothes, darning socks, and knitting. Most often, she was quilting. These precious quilts were hand sewn—every stitch. Each of her many grandchildren received one, usually on the occasion of marriage.

I remember unfolding mine. Intricate triangles and squares fitted into a full-size whole. Even when spread on the bed, however, I could never see the whole design at once because of its size with parts tucked under pillows or falling over the far side. It still reminds me of her. It is still beautiful to behold.

The Church's Unfolding Story on Sunday

Sunday unfolds for us the story of Christ, the story of the church. It is a story that is so big that we cannot tell it all at once.

It unfolds over time. It takes a whole year—the liturgical year—to let it unfold. Then we recall the importance of this central faith story by telling it again and again, liturgical year after liturgical year. Although it is the same story, we hear it in new ways because we grow, we are changed in the telling and retelling. That is why we do not take summers or vacations off from being church. We do not want to miss part of the storytelling.

Vatican II, Constitution on the Sacred Liturgy

By a tradition handed down from the apostles, which took its origin from the very day of Christ's resurrection, the church celebrates the paschal mystery every eighth day, . . . which day is appropriately called the Lord's day or Sunday. For on this day Christ's faithful are bound to come together so that, by hearing the word of God and taking part in the Eucharist, they may commemorate the suffering, resurrection, and glory of the Lord Jesus, giving thanks to God who "has given us a new birth into a living hope through the resurrection of Jesus Christ from the dead" (1 Pet 1:3). The Lord's Day is the original feast day, and it should be presented to the faithful and taught to them so that it may become in fact a day of rejoicing and of freedom from work. Other celebrations, unless they be truly of the greatest importance, shall not have precedence over Sunday, which is the foundation and kernel of the entire liturgical year. (106)

From the earliest days of the church, Sunday was *the* feast, *the* celebration for the followers of Jesus Christ. It still bears these names:

- the Day of Resurrection,
- the Lord's Day,
- the First Day of the Week,
- the Eighth Day.

The first members of this early church were rooted in Jewish life and prayer and history. Like their God who created, they rested on the seventh day, the Sabbath. But the resurrection of Christ Jesus shifted their attention from the last to that first day of the week. Eventually, they stopped gathering on Friday evening into Saturday to look back and give thanks for all of creation and God's work in the world. They were so astonished at what happened to Jesus, they had to do something new. They came together on Saturday during the night or on Sunday morning to celebrate this amazing new creation, this once dead but now risen Lord Jesus Christ. This was the day the Lord did a brand-new thing. Still today, on every Easter Sunday, we sing in the responsorial psalm: "This is the day the Lord has made; let us rejoice and be glad."

Universal Norms on the Liturgical Year and the General Roman Calendar

Holy Church celebrates the saving work of Christ on prescribed days in the course of the year with sacred remembrance. Each week, on the day called the Lord's Day, she commemorates the Resurrection of the Lord, which she also celebrates once a year in the great Paschal Solemnity, together with his blessed Passion. In fact, throughout the course of the year the Church unfolds the entire mystery of Christ and observes the birthdays of the Saints.

During the different periods of the liturgical year, in accord with traditional discipline, the Church completes the education of the faithful by means of spiritual and bodily devotional practices, instruction, prayer, works of penance, and works of mercy. (1)

The celebration of the Day of Resurrection launched these first believers into the new week to think and to act in new ways. That is why we still gather each Sunday to remember and give thanks. The former is a special kind of remembering, akin to the Jewish grasp of Passover: not just looking past, but believing, experiencing the past is present now, the God who saved us then is saving us today. The church uses *anamnesis* (a liturgical remembering that recalls the past as present reality) to describe this. It spills out into formal praying within each eucharistic prayer: "Do this in memory of me" and the proclamation of the "mystery of faith," with the acclamation of the assembly followed by a longer prayer focused on memorial and remembrance. Sunday is also a special time for giving thanks, the very meaning of Eucharist.

Every Sunday we ritually remember the dying and rising of Jesus Christ. We gather in community to hear Christ, the Word of God, speak to us today, to do Eucharist by giving thanks and praise, to eat his Body and drink his Blood, and to be sent to love and serve all week long. One Sunday, every so often, is not enough. It is Sunday after Sunday, week after week, season after season, year after year.

The parish may offer an assortment of formation events: occasional Bible study; occasional classes on theology; formal school year catechesis for the young; an annual mission or retreat; faith-sharing and prayer groups, especially in Advent or Lent; and baptism, confirmation, and marriage preparation. The parish may also recommend diocesan and regional events for the training and formation of Christians. But parish staffs know the participation in these events, as helpful as they are, includes only a smaller portion of the registered members. The greatest number—though, if truth be told, not 100 percent of parishioners—come only to Sunday Mass.

As important and timely as these many opportunities are, the weekly hour or so of Sunday Word and Eucharist is our primary formation event. It is formation that occurs in the midst of worship. Because liturgy is the first school of the church, that is why parish staffs pour time and energy and resources into every Sunday. It is the best thing we do. I have had the great pleasure

- to work with priests and deacons who say preaching is one of the most important things they do because it helps to break open Christ speaking to us today;

- to work with greeters who welcome all with hospitality and grace;

- to work with readers who bring their "A" game to the ambo, fully prepared to let Christ speak clearly;

- to work with liturgical musicians who struggle to choose music that is musically, ritually, and pastorally suitable for this day and this assembly;

- and to work with shapers of the ritual environment who manifest the feast and season without obscuring the centrality of what occurs at ambo and altar.

This is all very hard work—Sunday after Sunday, week after week.

Here we gather with other believers. Here Word and Eucharist are broken open. Here we sing of the goodness of God. Here these actions are applied to the lives we live and the world in which we live. Here we are charged to proclaim in the week that follows Christ's presence by our words and deeds.

The Church's Unfolding Story throughout the Year

Every Sunday does not look or sound exactly the same. Over the course of the year, we attend to part of the story of our redemption. Like the 75-foot maple tree in my yard whose trunk is too big to encircle in my arms, the Christ story is too big to grasp all at once. The weeks of the liturgical year, then, is the way that the church publicly prays and lives out and grasps the paschal mystery of the dead and risen Jesus Christ.

Vatican II, Constitution on the Sacred Liturgy

The minds of the faithful should be directed primarily toward the feasts of the Lord whereby the mysteries of salvation are celebrated throughout the year. For this reason, the Proper of the Seasons must be given due preference over the feasts of the saints so that the entire cycle of the mysteries of salvation may be suitably recalled. (108)

What makes up this year we call liturgical? The church usually describes the seasons of the year not in the order in which they are celebrated but in the order of importance. Here is that annual cycle following that latter way.

Paschal Triduum

The very heart of the liturgical year is the three days, the Sacred Paschal Triduum, the nexus between Lent and Easter Time. We count these days as do faithful Jews—dusk to dusk. It begins in the evening of Holy Thursday with the Mass of the Lord's Supper and ends with Evening Prayer II on the Sunday of Resurrection. The days and major celebrations are:

- *The Evening Mass of the Lord's Supper*, with the washing of feet, the procession of the faithful with gifts for the poor (the rubric, the rule, is very specific on that night), and the transfer of the Blessed Sacrament. Some time for adoration before the Eucharist follows.

- *The Celebration of the Passion of the Lord*, with the solemn intercessions, the exposition and adoration of the Holy Cross, and Communion. On this day, the genuflection, reserved to the Blessed Sacrament throughout the year, is also used to give honor to the cross this day. Some additional time for adoration before the cross follows.

- *The Easter Vigil in the Holy Night* has four parts. First, the blessing of the fire and preparation of the paschal candle, the procession, and the singing of the Easter proclamation. Second, the extended Liturgy of the Word, during which stories of redemption are read and heard and sung. Third, the baptismal liturgy, with calling on the saints, the blessing of water, baptism and confirmation, and the renewal of baptismal promises. Fourth, the Liturgy of the Eucharist with prayer and Communion.

- *Mass on Easter Day*

- *Evening Prayer*

To this list, we also add the preparation rites on Holy Saturday as the final part of purification and enlightenment with the elect (RCIA 185–205; Canada, 172–197). These rites are best seen not as private celebrations of the catechumenate team with the elect, but as truly public parish prayer on this day of paschal fasting in preparation for the great vigil.

Universal Norms on the Liturgical Year and the General Roman Calendar

Since Christ accomplished his work of human redemption and of the perfect glorification of God principally through his Paschal Mystery, in which by dying he destroyed our death, and by rising restored our life, the sacred Paschal Triduum of the Passion and Resurrection of the Lord shines forth as the high point of the entire liturgical year. Therefore the preeminence that Sunday has in the week, the Solemnity of Easter has in the liturgical year. (18)

Each and all of these liturgies make present the whole of the paschal mystery. We fight any mistaken urge to historicize individual elements in Christ's salvific life. We look to the supper and celebrate the whole paschal mystery. We look to the cross, to death, to burial and celebrate the whole paschal mystery. We listen to the great stories of salvation and the empty tomb and celebrate the whole paschal mystery. Jesus Christ is always present, whole and entire.

In treasuring Christ's life among us, we focus intently on initiation sacraments—how the water bath buries us in Christ and forms us as God's people, how the chrism oiling confirms the gifts of the Holy Spirit and completes baptism, how eating and drinking Blood and Body completes initiation and charges us to do Eucharist each succeeding Sunday so that we can live the Christian life all week.

Easter Time

This season comprises fifty days, seven weeks, and eight Sundays. It gives time to unpack the mysteries of baptism, confirmation, and the Eucharist. It gives us time to grasp in partial ways the huge reality of resurrected life in Christ.

> ## Universal Norms on the Liturgical Year and the General Roman Calendar
>
> The fifty days from the Sunday of Resurrection to Pentecost Sunday are celebrated in joy and exultation as one feast day, indeed as one "great Sunday." (22)

The *Rite of Christian Initiation of Adults* also sets this time aside for postbaptismal catechesis or mystagogy. "This is a time for the community and the neophytes together to grow in deepening their grasp of the paschal mystery and in making it part of their lives through meditation on the Gospel, sharing in the eucharist, and doing the works of charity" (RCIA 244; Canada, 234). The RCIA defines mystagogy as "a fuller and more effective understanding of mysteries through the Gospel message they have learned and above all through their experience of the sacraments they have received" (245; Canada, 235).

We are in this together. Neophytes help to shape us, we shape them, and we are all shaped by the dead and risen Christ in his word and meal and activity in our lives.

> ## Pope Francis, Audience with Participants in the Plenary of the Congregation for Divine Worship and the Discipline of the Sacraments
>
> In order for the liturgy to fulfil its formative and transforming function, it is necessary that the pastors and the laity be introduced to their meaning and symbolic language, including art, song and music in the service of the mystery celebrated, even

silence. The Catechism of the Catholic Church itself adopts the mystagogical way to illustrate the liturgy, valuing its prayers and signs. Mystagogy: this is a suitable way to enter the mystery of the liturgy, in the living encounter with the crucified and risen Lord. Mystagogy means discovering the new life we have received in the People of God through the Sacraments, and continually rediscovering the beauty of renewing it. (February 14, 2019)

Concerning this work of postbaptismal catechesis, this work of mystagogy, it is less about adding extra sessions each week to deliver more teaching and sign up for church-related jobs. That is the work of the earlier period of the catechumenate. It is more about parish planners seeking homiletic, musical, ministerial, and visual ways to unpack and extend this paschal feast, this great Sunday all the way through Pentecost. In other words, the primary ongoing formation of neophytes—and the faithful, too—takes place within, not outside of, the Sunday Masses of Easter Time (RCIA 247; Canada, 237).

This mystagogy (exploring the mystical presence of Jesus Christ the Lord yesterday, today, and forever) is a different style of catechetical formation. It helps us with careful guidance:

- to recall and reflect on ritual experience,

- to name evidence of God and Christ and Spirit active in our lives and the impact this has on the church's presence in the world,

- and to chart ways to strengthen or bring change to daily living.

We have permission to use the Easter Year A Lectionary readings each time we do this postbaptismal catechesis with neophytes (RCIA 247; Canada, 237), either on the Easter Sundays during the other liturgical years or when full initiation is celebrated, with the diocesan bishop's permission, outside of an Easter Vigil.

This is not the only instance for such permission. Sometimes the cycle of Scripture readings is so important and suitable that specific texts are given for certain celebrations. For example, whenever the three scrutinies are celebrated, the Lenten readings of the Third, Fourth, and Fifth Sundays from Year A must always be used (RCIA 146; Canada, 133, and *Lectionary for Mass*, 745–747). Whenever a marriage or a funeral is celebrated, readings are chosen from a collection specific to each celebration (except when marriage is celebrated within a Sunday Mass with parishioners). It is the same for confirmation and for ordination and a host of other ritual celebrations.

Why would the church give this permission? When Scripture is read aloud in liturgy, Christ himself speaks to us this day. The church selects certain passages to let Christ address more directly what is being celebrated. We read aloud and hear again the import of baptism when we baptize new members into Christ. We read aloud and hear again the impact of resurrected life when we pour ourselves into Easter living.

Lectionary for Mass, Introduction

In the celebration of the Liturgy the word of God is not announced in only one way nor does it always stir the hearts of the hearers with the same efficacy. Always, however, Christ is present in his word, as he carries out the mystery of salvation, he sanctifies humanity and offers the Father perfect worship. (4)

Lent

For those of us old enough to have lived the church's life prior to the reforms of the Second Vatican Council, we have had to retool our understanding and, perhaps, practice of Lent. At that time, our major if not only focus was to turn our lives around, to fast, to abstain, to sacrifice, and to do penance. It was worthy work.

> ## Universal Norms on the Liturgical Year and the General Roman Calendar
>
> Lent is ordered to preparing for the celebration of Easter, since the Lenten liturgy prepares for celebration of the Paschal Mystery both catechumens, by the various stages of Christian Initiation, and the faithful, who recall their own Baptism and do penance. (27)

With the restoration of the baptismal catechumenate and the reform of the liturgy, the church returned our focus of Lent to its older and proper intent. First, we turn our attention to the elected catechumens, those named on the First Sunday of Lent to celebrate the Easter sacraments during the coming vigil. We are charged to accompany them, to pray for and with them, to give them good examples of Lenten living. Because we see them, with our help, turn from evil and be strengthened by mighty prayer, we say, in so many words, "Oh, my God. Looking at them makes me look at my own life. Seeing them in the final stages of preparation for baptism makes me want to review my own baptismal status. What needs renewal, refreshment, restoration in me and in us, in the church and in the world?" This is the secondary intent of Lent. We are renewed by spending the Forty Days with those who will be made new in the font during the night of Easter.

For catechumenal ministers, this season also provides a different style of catechesis and formation. It is not a continuation of the period of the catechumenate training and formation, or worse, "catch-up catechesis" on the stuff missed in the preceding months because the period was perhaps too short. It is purification and enlightenment formation rooted in intensive focus on the scrutinies and presentations by preparation, celebration, and reflection (RCIA 138–139; Canada, 125–26).

Christmas Time

These celebrations of the first manifestations (note the plural) of Christ are bound to this shortest season. We celebrate two holy days—the Nativity of the Lord and Mary, the Mother of God—and usually three Sundays—Holy Family, Epiphany, and Baptism of the Lord. This is the pre-public life of Jesus that leads us from manifestation of God-with-us to only some to manifestation to all.

Universal Norms on the Liturgical Year and the General Roman Calendar

After the annual celebration of the Paschal Mystery, the Church has no more ancient custom than celebrating the memorial of the Nativity of the Lord and of his first manifestations, and this takes place in Christmas Time. (32)

Although the *Lectionary for Mass*, at the beginning of the section of readings for Ordinary Time, states that "The First Sunday in Ordinary Time is the Feast of the Baptism of the Lord," the readings are, in fact, included in the section for Christmas Time. Both the Roman Missal and the Universal Norms on the Liturgical Year and the General Roman Calendar include this feast in Christmas Time. It is the last celebration of that season. Ordinary Time begins on the following day.

The challenge to catechumenal formation in this short season is to maintain dismissal and suitable formation around each day. The dismissal of catechumens, which is the church's duty to provide even during the big Christmas Masses, can have a subtle impact on some less than regular attendees.

Advent

This season of Advent continues the attention on the second coming of Christ that was the drive of the preceding few weeks during the end of Ordinary Time. We pray for this next coming confident that it is and will come because Christ came once already. Halfway through the season, we shift our focus to recall the first coming. Advent, then, proclaims that because Christ came first as a human, one like us in all things but sin, we trust and believe he will come again. It is our prayer.

Universal Norms on the Liturgical Year and the General Roman Calendar

Advent has a twofold character, for it is a time of preparation for the Solemnities of Christmas, in which the First Coming of the Son of God to humanity is remembered, and likewise a time when, by remembrance of this, minds and hearts are led to look forward to Christ's Second Coming at the end of time. For these two reasons, Advent is a period for devout and expectant delight. (39)

December shifts to a time when ministers and the church building are dressed differently, with deep purples and fewer floral displays. It is in sharp contrast to the "green" Sundays of summer and fall in Ordinary Time. For catechumenal ministers, adding the Rite of Acceptance into the order of catechumens to this mix may be too much for the parish and the season. It has never been required during these days. Let catechumens revel in comings past, present, and future.

Ordinary Time

The bulk of the liturgical year is Ordinary Time, counted time. While in the major seasons, we speak of Sundays *of* Advent, Sundays *of* Lent, Sundays *of* Easter, we now deal with Sundays *in* Ordinary Time. That is because we do not focus on a single aspect of Christ and his paschal mystery. We focus instead on all of it a bit at a time.

Universal Norms on the Liturgical Year and the General Roman Calendar

Apart from those seasons having their own distinctive character, thirty-three or thirty-four weeks remain in the yearly cycle that do not celebrate a specific aspect of the mystery of Christ. Rather, especially on the Sundays, they are devoted to the mystery of Christ in all its aspects. This period is known as Ordinary Time. (43)

It is celebrated in two segments: five to nine Sundays in the winter between Christmas Time and Lent (dependent on the moveable date of Easter) and the much longer period of summer through fall.

These counted Sundays explore the holiness of the church by unfolding some dimension of the reign and kingdom of God. In so doing, it unwraps a specific part of the mystery of Christ dead and risen.

Here is a truth. As Catholics, we do not take summer off. We still gather each Sunday, even when away on vacation. Otherwise, we would miss some essential proclamation. We would miss important parts of the ever-unfolding story. Those involved in the parish baptismal catechumenate ministry have the duty to continue the training and formation of catechumens through the summer weeks. They have the right to Sunday Word, to weekly dismissal, and to summer activities of formation, parish life and service (as spelled out in RCIA 75) just as the parish has the duty to provide them. It may be simpler in the summer, when the living is easy, but it is weekly.

The Importance of Attending to the Whole Liturgical Year

In telling the story of Christ, the liturgical year tells the story of life in Christ, it tells the story of the church, and it tells our story. It is told in its own distinctive way. There is a system, a method, a syllabus, an agenda. But it is not organized like a textbook or a catechism or a degree program. It does not take the hierarchical order of the Nicene Creed, nor does it address an important topic only once.

The Roman Missal inherited from the Council of Trent (1545–1563) had a single year format. The Sunday gospels came mostly from Matthew and there were few readings from the Old Testament. The bishop was empowered to set out an annual Sunday sermon plan. It was a way to provide formation for the faithful coming to Sunday Mass. It may or may not have been in harmony with the readings or the seasons. We used this Missal, with only modest changes, for nearly four hundred years.

General Instruction of the Roman Missal

The homily is part of the Liturgy and is highly recommended, for it is necessary for the nurturing of the Christian life. It should be an explanation of some aspect of the readings from Sacred Scripture or of another text from the Ordinary or the Proper of the Mass of the day and should take into account both the mystery being celebrated and the particular needs of the listeners. (65)

The Second Vatican Council gave us a new Missal with a new Lectionary plan rooted in a three-year cycle of readings expanding to four biblical texts for each Sunday:

- Reading from the Old Testament or from the Acts of the Apostles during Easter Time
- Psalm sung in responsorial fashion
- Reading from the New Testament
- Reading from a gospel

Preaching shifted from a sermon on almost any topic to a homily with a directed focus. Now, preachers pay attention to the aspect of the mystery of Christ and the needs of the gathered assembly this Sunday using any of the following:

- something from the Word of God proclaimed

- something from the Ordinary, that is, repeatable Mass texts

- something from the Proper, that is, specific texts of the Mass of the day

Let us be clear. The church shifted from a structure more academically or hierarchically organized (as the Creed is ordered) to a structure that dances back and forth within aspects of the great paschal mystery, the saving presence of Christ in our midst. Instead of treating penance and forgiveness all at once, for example, it is dealt with a handful of times over the course of the year a bit at a time. Instead of treating the importance of Mary to the church all at once, she is addressed throughout the year as immaculately born, listening to and trusting God, Mother of God, mother of great sorrows, and assumed into heaven.

Let us be clear. The Creed is important. We proclaim it each Sunday in Nicene or Apostles' form. It gives us a hierarchical ordering from God to death-heaven-hell. It gives us a proclamation of basic belief. But recall, it is presented to elected catechumens in Lent *after* catechumenal training is complete as the thoroughgoing summary of their initiatory formation.

Let us be clear. The Sunday textbook for training and formation is not a catechism but rather the Lectionary, the Missal, and the liturgical songs used on Sundays.

In telling the story of Christ, the liturgical year tells the story of life in Christ, it tells the story of the church, and it tells our story.

Practical Tips

Living the liturgical year must be intentional. Otherwise it will slip by and we may miss an important aspect of Christ.

Seasonal Focus

Advent and Christmas Time are easier, especially with children in the home. Make use of the Advent wreath, the Jesse tree, the Christmas tree and crèche and gifts. Bring holy water home especially for Lent and Easter Time. Palm branches (from Palm Sunday) and blessed candles (from the Presentation of the Lord on February 2) can also have prominent places to aid prayer.

Color

A tie or scarf or sweater in the liturgical color of the season can help each person to focus on the part of the liturgical year being celebrated with the church. Tablecloths in meeting rooms will also draw attention to the time of year. Use as a guide what the General Instruction of the Roman Missal, 346, provides as guidance concerning vestments:

- violet or purple in Advent—darker hues fit the season best;
- white in Christmas Time as well as the many solemnities of the Lord and of the Virgin Mary;
- violet or purple in Lent—redder hues fit the season;
- green in Ordinary Time;
- and red for Palm Sunday, Good Friday, Pentecost, and feast days of the apostles, evangelists, and martyrs.

Bible and Spiritual Reading

Do some reading that attends to the season. Perhaps the Prophet Isaiah in Advent, Acts of the Apostles in Easter Time, Matthew in Year A, Mark in Year B, and Luke in Year C. Look to the parish pamphlet rack and bulletin inserts as well as the diocesan paper or magazine for help to delve into the seasons. See the following Helpful Resources section for a short booklist.

Helpful Resources

Universal Norms on the Liturgical Year and the General Roman Calendar (UNLYC).

> This document is short. It is included in the front part of *The Roman Missal, Third Edition*, and provides the official descriptions of Sunday and the liturgical year. It is also found in the following documents.

> Liturgy Documentary Series 14. *The General Instruction of the Roman Missal including Norms for the Distribution and Reception of Holy Communion under Both Kinds in the Dioceses of the United States of America and Universal Norms on the Liturgical Year and the General Roman Calendar.* Washington, DC: United States Conference of Catholic Bishops, 2011. Pages 151–75.

> *The Liturgy Documents: Essential Documents for Parish Worship, Fifth Edition.* Chicago: Liturgy Training Publications, 2012. Pages 201–20.

Lectionary for Mass for Use in the Dioceses of the United States of America, Second Typical Edition. Various publishers, Volume I (Sundays and Solemnities), 1998; Volumes II–IV (weekdays and special rites), 2002.

> See Introduction, Chapter V, Description of the Order of Readings, 92–110. Following the order of the liturgical year and the Lectionary, it provides the focus of the chosen readings for each season.

Lectionary, third edition following the second typical edition (for Canada). Ottawa: Canadian Conference of Catholic Bishops, 1992 and 1994. Volumes: Sunday and Solemnities, 1992; Weekdays A and B, 1994.

> See Introduction, Chapter V, Description of the Order of Readings, 92–110. Following the order of the liturgical year and the Lectionary, it provides the focus of the chosen readings for each season.

The Year of Grace Liturgical Calendar. Chicago: Liturgy Training Publications, annual.

> This annual publication, in handout and poster sizes, presents a dated wheel of the current liturgical year and contemporary images to draw us into the beauty of Christ. A Spanish edition is also available.

Kathy Coffey, Donna M. Crilly, Mary G. Fox, Mary Ellen Hynes, Julie M. Krakora, Corinna Laughlin, and Robert C. Rabe. *Companion to the Calendar, Second Edition: A Guide to the Saints, Seasons, and Holidays of the Year.* Chicago: Liturgy Training Publications, 2012.

> This fleshes out both the seasons and the days described in the Universal Norms on the Liturgical Year and the General Roman Calendar.

Gabe Huck and Gerald T. Chinchar. *Liturgy with Style and Grace.* Chicago: Liturgy Training Publications, 1998. Revised 2018.

> Unit 5, Days and Seasons, provides a concise overview of the liturgical year season by season with some reflective questions.

Many periodicals provide some description of and guidance for the liturgical seasons.

> *At Home with the Word.* Annual. Liturgy Training Publications.
>
> *Catholic Updates.* Monthly four-page newsletter on various topics. Liguori Publications.
>
> *Give Us This Day: Daily Prayer for Today's Catholics.* Monthly. Liturgical Press.
>
> *Living Liturgy: Spirituality, Celebration, and Catechesis for Sundays and Solemnities.* Annual. Liturgical Press.
>
> *Sourcebook for Sundays, Seasons, and Weekdays.* Annual. Liturgy Training Publications.
>
> *Sunday Prayer for Catholics.* Annual. Liturgy Training Publications.
>
> *The Word Among Us.* Monthly. The Word Among Us Press.

The Liturgical Year

is the way the	CHURCH
publicly	PRAYS
and	LIVES OUT
the	PASCHAL MYSTERY
of the	DEAD AND RISEN JESUS CHRIST.

TIME	CHRISTIAN LIFE	THEOLOGY & LITURGY
ADVENT • 4 weeks	• joyful expectation • spiritual longing • preparation for the end time	2 COMINGS OF CHRIST • first—Incarnation • second—end of time
CHRISTMAS TIME • about 2½ weeks • octave • Epiphany of the Lord • Baptism of the Lord	• hope • God-with-us	THE PROMISED ONE • is born in Jesus • is manifested to all
ORDINARY TIME • 5 to 9 weeks	HOLINESS OF THE CHURCH	KINGDOM OF GOD
LENT • 40 (44) days • Sundays in the count • Ash Wednesday • ends before Evening Mass of the Lord's Supper	• beginning • preparation • pregnancy	RENEWAL/ CONVERSION • final steps to full Christian initiation • reaffirm baptism and do penance—fast, pray, and give alms
PASCHAL TRIDUUM • The three days • meal • cross • tomb • empty tomb	**BIRTH of the CHRISTIAN** • baptism • confirmation • Eucharist	**PASCHAL MYSTERY** • passion, death, resurrection, ascension, and sitting at the right hand of God
EASTER TIME • 50 days • ends with Pentecost	MISSION of the CHRISTIAN • What happens to Jesus happens to us.	"THE GREAT SUNDAY" • revels in the GREAT MYSTERY
ORDINARY TIME • 24 to 26 weeks • last Sunday is Our Lord Jesus Christ, King of the Universe	HOLINESS OF THE CHURCH	KINGDOM OF GOD • unfolds how it is manifested

Chapter 4

The Ongoing Catechetical Reform

Story: Caring for Lawn and Garden

Before my sixtieth birthday, I used a push-reel lawn mower. I had to mow frequently during the height of the growing season. Although it was the only one in the neighborhood, I told myself the exercise was good for me. I was comfortable with this eco-friendly device. For a long time, I did not want to change methods. Because it had no grass catcher, it also meant raking and bagging leaves all fall for city pick up. When I inherited my mother's leaf shredder, I was able to start a compost heap and add shredded leaves to the gardens. Whenever I needed grass clippings to properly layer the compost, my neighbor was more than happy to give me what I needed instead of paying to have it hauled away. Over time, I reduced and then stopped buying mulch, peat moss, and composted soil.

At sixty years, I bought a gas mower with a bagging attachment. It was not belt driven, so I still get some exercise. But yard work shifted again. I stopped putting bags of yard waste at the curb. Composting increased. I added two rain barrels. I planted more vegetables, and surplus tomatoes always found happy homes.

The end was the same: a tended lawn, healthy crops, beautiful flowers. The methods changed, however, becoming more organic, attending to the annual cycle, practical needs, and my own age and abilities.

Caring for the Instruction of the Faithful

Catechesis has a long history in the life of the Catholic Church. It adapted incrementally to the times and needs of the people until the more seismic shifts of the Second Vatican Council's reforms. With the advent of the printing press, in the mid-1400s, popular catechisms by Reformers and Catholics alike followed for the instruction of the faithful. A key example is Martin Luther's *Small Catechism*, published in 1529, for the training of children in simple ways, often with questions and answers, by the head of the household. The Council of Trent, in one of its responses to the Reformers, commissioned the first universal *Roman Catechism* in 1566. It was primarily written, however, for improving the theological understanding of the clergy in their pastoral care of parishioners.

In the United States, there was an earnest desire as early as 1829 to provide a practical catechism for the instruction of children suited to the needs of a relatively new nation and growing church population. Finally, in 1885, *A Catechism of Christian Doctrine Prepared and Enjoined by Order of the Third Council of Baltimore* was issued. Commonly called the *Baltimore Catechism*, it was primarily written by one priest in about ten days. It underwent local diocesan and publisher editions, sometimes shortening the original 421 questions, for example, or supplying maps, glossaries, and prayers. The focus remained on the instruction of children. Revisions made in the twentieth century involved hundreds of consultants and took years to write and edit, resulting in four volumes for age-specific use.

The *Baltimore Catechism* was part of my formation, both before and after entering Sacred Heart Catholic School in the mid-1950s, especially in preparation for First Communion in the second grade and confirmation in the fourth. I can still recite from memory some of the early questions and answers I learned then by rote.

Until the Second Vatican Council, the *Roman Catechism* and the *Baltimore Catechism* remained in use, the former as a guide for clergy, the latter for the instruction of children. Officially, little was provided for the formation of adults.

Caring for the Word of God in All Its Forms

Although the bishops at the Second Vatican Council discussed the composition of a new catechism, they shifted their direction to the broader approach of seeking guidelines, recommendations, and procedures addressing all the faithful. Specifically, *Christus Dominus*, the Decree on the Pastoral Office of Bishops in the Church (1965), called for the compiling of

> a directory for the catechetical instruction of the christian people in which the fundamental principles of this instruction and its organization will be dealt with and the preparation of books relating to it. (44)

This task was assigned to the Sacred Congregation for the Clergy. This put in motion a broad consultation in reforming catechetical processes and formation.

Methods and materials shifted with the council. The *United States Catholic Catechism for Adults*, called for by the universal *Catechism of the Catholic Church*, formally replaced the editions of the *Baltimore Catechism*. But the basic goal remained: informed Catholics would make other life-long, well-formed Catholics who are able to live the apostolic life with faith and vigor. As public and secondary education became more common, the intent for religious education moved beyond a child-only approach.

In the words of Pope John XXIII, the coming Second Vatican Council was to open the windows of the church to the world and let both the church more effectively affect the world and the world impact the ministry of the church without diluting her mission.

Even before the council formally closed in December of 1965, the phrase "participation of the faithful" was taking hold. It was apparent, first of all, in the gradual reform of the liturgy. This participation also spilled over to assistance with education, catechesis, liturgical ministry, social welfare involvement, and governance.

A review of the key post–Vatican II documents details our growth in understanding the place of catechesis within the larger ministry of the Word of God. We see how it is rooted in Sacred Scripture, in tradition, in the liturgy of the church, in the faith community, and in works of charity, justice, and mercy.

It took the Apostolic See, through the Sacred Congregation for the Clergy, six years after the close of the council to issue the first catechetical document. The *General Catechetical Directory* (GCD) of 1971 was developed with the help of the conferences of bishops throughout the world. It situated catechesis within the larger ministry of the word. A review of the table of contents itself reflects changes to the content and methods of formation from both the *Roman Catechism* and the *Baltimore Catechism*.

It began by addressing the characteristics of the current situation, first in the world and in the church. The next part focused on the ministry of the word and its intimate connection to revelation, Jesus Christ (the spoken Word of God), preaching, Scripture, and faith. Only then did it address the nature, purpose, and efficacy of catechesis within the context of the word and evangelization. It detailed the forms and functions of catechesis within this pastoral mission of the church.

The next part addressed the specifics of the Christian message. Of note was the list of the most outstanding elements of the Christian message. This hierarchical ordering, like the order of beliefs in the Nicene Creed, dominated universal and national documents until the *Catechism of the Catholic Church* would call for another shift twenty-three years later in 1994 (more on that shift later).

Part 4 addressed methodology, the function of the catechist, the preference for deductive learning, and the value of attending to experience to shape learning.

Part 5 addressed age level formation from infancy to old age—a significant and formal shift from the older catechisms. In light of all that preceded, the final part addressed formation in the ministry of catechetics, aids, organization, and coordination of the catechetical efforts.

This universal document was not the final word. It served as the necessary guide for each national conference to formulate its own local document adapted to the genius and needs of its people. In the United States, it took three documents addressing only partial elements of the GCD to arrive at *Sharing the Light of Faith: National Catechetical Directory for Catholics of the United States* (NCD), in 1977 and updated in 1979.

Of particular note in the NCD is the American shift from the narrower focus of previous conference documents on "educational ministry" and "religious education" to the broader "catechesis" and "catechetical ministry." It stressed that the task of catechesis is the fostering of mature faith. It stressed that because the church is a worshipping community, faith and worship are ultimately intertwined. It stressed that initiation occurs in stages and that the *Rite of Christian Initiation of Adults* provides a norm for all catechetical and liturgical practice. It stressed that the liturgical year is not a mere recalling of Christ's life on earth but, in unfolding the mystery of Christ on Sunday and in the seasons, it completes the formation of the faithful.

The *Catechism of the Catholic Church*, debated in the Second Vatican Council but deferred to the end of the twentieth century, was developed not only through broad consultation of national conferences, but by the help of the individual dioceses within the larger body of bishops. I recall the great joy and appreciation of Bishop Daniel Ryan at the broad participation the Diocese of Springfield in Illinois undertook at his direction and involvement in addressing the draft. The final document approved by Pope John Paul II in 1994 was appreciably different because of this world-wide effort.

Bear in mind that this catechism was never intended to be a textbook for adult formation, much less one for use as such in the baptismal catechumenate. It was assembled as a helpful compendium for bishops to assist them in their duty as first teacher and guardian of tradition. Secondarily, it could help all priests and those engaged in catechetical ministry. Finally, it could be "useful reading for all the Christian faithful."

In 1997, Rome issued the *General Directory for Catechesis* (GDC), a revision of the GCD twenty-six years earlier. While maintaining many of the helpful elements of the older document, it reflected a growth in understanding and maturity in the work of catechesis. It was influenced by two papal documents: *Evangelii Nuntiandi* on Evangelization in the Modern World (EN) by Pope Paul VI in 1975 and *Catechesi Tradendae* on Catechesis in our Time (CT) by Pope John Paul II in 1979. Each was a follow-up response to a preceding synod of bishops addressing the chosen topic.

Of significance in the GDC was the replacement of the list of outstanding elements of the Christian message (a hierarchical and dogmatic approach to formation) with use of the newly issued *Catechism of the Catholic Church*, which was structured on the four pillars of the profession of faith, the sacraments, the life of faith, and prayer in the life of faith. It was given as a guide to bishops, priests, and catechists to support catechesis, not as a textbook for doing catechesis.

Catechism of the Catholic Church

By design this Catechism does not set out to provide the adaptation of doctrinal presentations and catechetical methods required by the differences of culture, age, spiritual maturity, and social and ecclesial condition among all those to whom it is addressed. Such indispensable adaptations are the responsibility of particular catechisms and, even more, of those who instruct the faithful. (24)

Story: All Catechesis All the Time

Shortly after the good success of Jubilee 2003, the sesquicentennial of the Diocese of Springfield in Illinois, the diocesan staff begin wrestling with the request of Bishop George Lucas to address a more thorough approach to catechesis. The curia directors and associates floundered for a year and a half of meetings on the meaning, intent, and methods of this charge.

A mandatory "town hall" meeting for everyone from janitor to bishop was held during Advent, replacing the annual day of prayer. After a morning of interoffice small group conversation and large group reporting, the bishop made his first comments. He thanked all for attention to the task, commented on some specifics he heard, and took a deep breath.

He went on: I am a little nervous about what I will say next, but I trust you because of your past hard work. We are a big in area but small in staffing rural diocese with some limits on resources. I want you to stop doing some good things you are doing for the benefit of doing other good things needed now. Here is what I mean about catechesis all the time. Here is what I see as our new task for the benefit of the people of the diocese:

1. to foster a personal relationship with Jesus Christ,

2. always within a communal relationship with Jesus Christ,

3. animated by a living faith.

This must be the work of not just the Office for Catechesis, but of finance, insurance, support staff, that is, everyone.

That galvanized the work of the afternoon. We pledged ourselves to devise short and long-term plans for each office, listing what could be curtailed or stopped so that new and needed efforts could begin. The ten diverse offices in the Department for Catechetical Services in which I worked also began regular meetings for study of the catechetical tradition of the church along with regular prayer and faith sharing to help this effort.

Catechesis in Our Own Day

While working on the national adaptations of the universal GDC, the US bishops issued *Our Hearts Were Burning Within Us: A Pastoral Plan for Adult Faith Formation in the United States* in 1999. In this small text of seventy-one pages, they wrote for a broad spectrum of parish and diocesan leaders on the primacy and centrality of adult faith formation. This formation must be at the very heart of all catechetical vision and practice. It is worthy reading for all those involved in baptismal catechumenate formation.

United States Conference of Catholic Bishops, *Our Hearts Were Burning Within Us*

Adult faith formation, by which people consciously grow in the life of Christ through experience, reflection, prayer, and study, must be "the *central task* in [this] catechetical enterprise," becoming "the axis around which revolves the catechesis of childhood and adolescence as well as that of old age." This can be done specifically through developing in adults a better understanding and participation in the full sacramental life of the Church. (p. 2)

This explicit shift away from a child-only approach to the centrality of adult formation is a huge undertaking. Some key points of this document follow:

- A living faith grows and develops over time, learns from experience, adapts to changing conditions, and trusts the work of the Holy Spirit season after season (pp. 16–17).

- A living faith is maintained by participating actively in liturgy; reading the Bible, tradition, and the documents of the church frequently; personal prayer; doing the works of justice and service to the poor; and fulfilling human obligations to family and society by love of God and neighbor (p. 17).

- Adult formation is guided and directed by these goals: (1) invite and enable ongoing conversion to Jesus in holiness of life, (2) promote and support active membership in the Christian community, and (3) call and prepare adults to act as disciples in mission to the world (pp. 22–24).

- The bishops implore the use of the baptismal catechumenate as an inspiring model for all catechesis, citing GDC 59, 68, and 88–91 (p. 26).

- A living, explicit, and fruitful faith requires an interrelated and necessary knowledge of the faith, liturgical life, moral formation, prayer (in addition to liturgical prayer), communal life, and missionary spirit (pp. 28–33).

- Concrete approaches must be diverse because no single one meets everyone's needs (p. 34).

- This multifaceted approach must use liturgy, family-centered or home-centered activities, small groups, large groups, and individual activities (pp. 34–38).

- Since the primary experience of church for most Catholics is the parish, the parish is the curriculum. The success of adult faith formation rests in the quality and total fabric of parish life. Involvement in ministry and powerful preaching are key (pp. 40–41).

- Life-long involvement in Christian formation and in the life of Christ must be intentional aspects for shaping parish culture (pp. 42–43).

- Catechists of adults must be people of faith and prepared for the many aspects of faith formation (pp. 51–52).

United States Conference of Catholic Bishops, *Our Hearts Were Burning Within Us*

It is not enough for catechists to know their subjects. They also need the competence to animate a shared journey with other adults, the ability to relate authentic Catholic faith to real-life circumstances, the ability to guide them in prayer and through spiritual experiences, and the craft to integrate divergent tendencies into the full faith and life of the Church. It is essential that catechists witness in their own lives the truth of the faith they are communicating. This requires a love for people, a passion for catechesis, effective interpersonal and community-building skills, respect for different adult learning styles, the ability to communicate and explore the Gospel with

> others using active and engaging methods appropriate to the learners and to the content, and the flexibility to adapt to ever-changing circumstances. (p. 51)

The term "catechesis" has a long history in Christian usage. It has greatly evolved. It is distinguished, though not separated from the following (p. 52).

- *Evangelization:* the proclamation of the Good News of Jesus Christ for the first time.

- *Re-evangelization or new evangelization:* the ongoing proclamation for those who have forgotten the proclamation.

- *Initiatory or basic catechesis* for catechumens and candidates completing their initiation.

- *Formal religious education* for a host of situations, moving beyond basic elements of faith with more systematic and specialized courses.

- *Postbaptismal or permanent or continuing catechesis* for all Christians to constantly nourish and deepen their faith throughout their lives.

- *Informal occasions for faith awareness in God's presence*, "which arise in fragmentary and incidental ways in the daily life of adults."

It also took twenty-six years, after intensive consultation, for the American conference to issue its own revised directory. The *National Directory for Catechesis* (NDC) of 2005 built on the improvements of the GDC of 1997, the second universal edition.

The opening chapter provides an overview of some contemporary cultural and religious factors that have an influence on catechesis in the United States. Consistent with the view of the Second Vatican Council, this attention to the world in which we live sets a context for the next three chapters:

• Catechesis within the church's mission of evangelization,

• the faith of the church,

• and divine and human methodology.

Chief learnings, especially for catechumenal ministers, are the relationship of evangelization and the ministry of the word, the relationship of initiatory and ongoing catechesis, and an attention to inculturation in proclaiming the Gospel. These are elements fostered and esteemed by the Second Vatican Council.

United States Conference of Catholic Bishops, *National Directory for Catechesis*

Initiatory catechesis cultivates the roots of faith, nurtures a distinctively Christian spiritual life, and prepares the person to be nourished at the table of Eucharist and in the ordinary life of the Christian community.

Initiatory catechesis incorporates those preparing for the sacraments of initiation into the Christian community that knows, lives, celebrates, and bears witness to the faith. The richness of this initiatory catechesis should serve to inspire other forms of catechesis. (2.D)

Section 29 details the elements of divine and human methodology essential for catechetical formation. We learn faith not just from the delivery of information but through human experience and by discipleship. We are formed within the Christian community and the Christian family. We are shaped through the living witness of catechists and learning by heart. Concerning this, however, the NDC cautions that "the content of faith cannot be reduced to formulas that are repeated without being properly understood" (2.F). This is a shift long in the making from the first edition of the *Baltimore Catechism*. Finally, we are formed by making a commitment to living the Christian life learned through an apprenticeship methodology. Hear the echoes of RCIA 75 and 78 and the Decree on the Church's Missionary Activity, *Ad Gentes*, 14.

Spending time with the fifth chapter on catechesis in a worshipping community is worthy study time for ministers who work with the baptismal catechumenate. It addresses the intimate relationship between catechesis and liturgy, the relationship of communal and personal prayer, and the importance of the liturgical year and the sacred arts in all formation.

A story from my diocesan experience concerning this chapter: With the reception of a new bishop in 2010 and a restructuring of the diocesan staff two years later, the new and larger Department for Catechetical Services included nine directors and associates for the offices for Campus Ministry, Catechesis, Catholic Schools (two members), Lay Ministry Formation, Marriage and Family Life, Missions, Youth and Young Adults, and Worship and the Catechumenate. These were the personnel who most directly served the parishes with assistance in pastoral ministry.

With our new departmental title, we decided that study of the NDC would be essential for our work together. We raced through the first four chapters. We slowed down in discussing chapter 5 on catechesis in a worshipping community due in part to my chairing that part of our discussion, due in part to the line, "the baptismal catechumenate is the source of inspiration for all catechesis." Not just sacramental catechesis but *all* catechesis.

As much as I would have loved everyone in the department to be part of a parish RCIA team, none of them were, nor could they be because of distinctive and pressing diocesan duties. But we arrived at the conclusion that each of us, like every catechist and preacher, must have *informational competence* concerning the baptismal catechumenate. We worked on this for half a year.

In the first decade of the twenty-first century, the *United States Catholic Catechism for Adults* (USCCA) was approved, recognized by Rome, and published first in 2006 and in revised form in 2010. This catechism for the United States follows the four parts of the *Catechism of the Catholic Church*. It is divided into thirty-six chapters and concludes with a glossary, traditional Catholic prayers, and a short list for further reading. Unlike the universal catechism, it employs a narrative and conversational style. The distinctive structure of each chapter of the book is:

- story or lesson of faith,

- teaching—its foundation and application,

- sidebars,

- relationship of Catholic teaching to culture,

- questions for discussion,

- doctrinal statements,

- and meditation and prayer.

Practical Tips

Reading, pondering, and attending to the key points of *Our Hearts Were Burning Within Us: A Pastoral Plan for Adult Faith Formation in the United States* is worthy and practical work.

Helpful Resources
About Catechetical Methods

Thomas H. Groome. *Sharing Faith: A Comprehensive Approach to Religious Education and Pastoral Ministry—The Way of Shared Praxis*. New York: HarperSanFrancisco, 1991.

> Part II details the steps known as "Groome's Shared Christian Praxis." It has five movements of "Focusing Activity": (1) Naming/Expressing "Present Praxis," (2) Critical Reflection on Present Action, (3) Making Accessible Christian Story and Vision, (4) Dialectical Hermeneutic to Appropriate Christian Story and Vision, (5) Decision/Response for Lived Christian Faith. Although this method is most helpful for faith formation, this is not an easy book to read. Contact local or regional master catechists and diocesan offices for catechesis, formation, or worship for a simple and adequate training method.

Kathleen Hughes. *Saying Amen: A Mystagogy of Sacrament*. Chicago: Liturgy Training Publications, 1999.

> A foundational book for understanding and doing mystagogical catechesis. Chapter 1 addresses mystagogy as method and provides seven key characteristics for this theological reflection. Chapter 2, on paying attention, addresses active participation, celebrating liturgy well, contemplation, and liturgical engagement. Beginning with Christian initiation of adults, the remaining eight chapters apply the method to other dimensions of the sacramental life.

Gilbert Ostdiek. *Catechesis for Liturgy: A Program for Parish Involvement*. Portland, OR: OCP, 1986.

> Chapter 1 nicely summarizes three models for Christian formation: mystagogical catechesis, Groome's shared Christian praxis, and the author's method used in the book: *attending* to what we and others experience, *reflecting* on what our experience and that of others means, *applying* what we have learned to future celebrations.

Roc O'Connor, SJ. *In the Midst of Our Storms: Opening Ourselves to Christ in the Liturgy*. Chicago: Liturgy Training Publications, 2015.

> Provides a poetic and spiritual method to engage more deeply in the paschal mystery and the liturgy of the church.

Paprocki, Joseph and D. Todd Williamson. *Great Is the Mystery: Encountering the Formational Power of the Liturgy*. Chicago: Liturgy Training Publications, 2012.

> This book consists of twenty-five chapters gathered in four parts: (1) proclaiming the mystery of sign, symbol, and ritual; (2) proclaiming the mystery of the church at prayer; (3) proclaiming the mystery of the eucharistic liturgy; and (4) proclaiming the mystery of the liturgical year. A chapter, in treating a topic, gives examples from life experience and cites documents. It concludes with suggestions for ministry and daily living and questions for reflection and discussion on liturgical ministry, catechesis, RCIA, and general adult audiences.

Joe Paprocki. *Beyond the Catechist's Toolbox: Catechesis That Not Only Informs but Also Transforms*. Chicago: Loyola Press, 2013.

> Stresses the need to know the language of mystery to do catechesis. Provides a five-stage method for doing catechetical sessions: Preliminaries, the ENGAGE Step, the EXPLORE Step, the REFLECT Step, and the RESPOND Step.

Some Key Documents on Catechesis

The chart below shows both the progressive development of the understanding and practices of catechesis as well as the interplay of universal and national publications. Although the latter is only reflected by the works in the United States, similar work also took place in Canada.

Universal Publications	National Publications, United States
Council of Trent, *Roman Catechism*, 1566. • In response to the Reformers, this first universal catechism aimed to assist clergy with sound theological formularies.	
	Third Council of Baltimore, *Baltimore Catechism*, 1885. • Patterned on Robert Bellarmine's *Small Catechism* (1614) for children in Q&A format.
Second Vatican Council, *Christus Dominus*, Decree on the Pastoral Office of Bishops in the Church (CD), October 28, 1965. • Calls for a new approach, with a directory rather than a catechism, to provide directives and guidelines, recommendations and procedures rather than answers to questions.	
Second Vatican Council, *Ad Gentes*, Decree on the Church's Missionary Activity (AG), December 7, 1965. • Directs that catechumenal formation be an extended apprenticeship, a gradual formation rooted in the life of faith, liturgy, and charity as a concern of the entire community of believers.	

Universal Publications	National Publications, United States

Sacred Congregation for the Clergy, *General Catechetical Directory* (GCD), 1971.
  • This first directory called for and assisted the development of national directories and, eventually, catechisms. Of note is chapter 2, part 2, providing a list of the more outstanding elements of the Christian message.

Sacred Congregation for Divine Worship, *Ordo Initiationis Christianae Adultorum*, typical edition, January 6, 1972.
  • Although not a catechetical document but a liturgical book, it lays out the norms and methods for catechumenal formation leading to the sacraments of Christian initiation.

National Conference of Catholic Bishops (NCCB), *To Teach as Jesus Did* (TJD), November 1972.
  • Restricting to the narrower focus of religious education, it listed the importance of prayer, participation in liturgy, and familiarity with the Bible as three essential themes. It modestly expanded the basic teachings of the GCD.

NCCB, *Basic Teachings for Catholic Religious Education* (BT), January 11, 1973.
  • A national consultation resulted in additional guidance for Catholic educators. Of note: learning or total Catholic education is a lifelong experience with interlocking dimensions of message, fellowship, and service.

Universal Publications	National Publications, United States
	Rite of Christian Initiation of Adults (RCIA), provisional text for interim use in the dioceses of the United States, 1974. • This first translation, without any local adaptations, helped the local churches to begin the transition to a renewed method for catechumenal formation.
Paul VI, *Evangelii Nuntiandi*, Apostolic Exhortation on Evangelization in the Modern World (EN), December 8, 1975. • Christ is the center of evangelization, with catechesis holding an important though partial aspect of this broader effort. Inculturation, called for in the Constitution on the Sacred Liturgy, is an essential dimension of this essential work.	
	NCCB, *Sharing the Light of Faith: National Catechetical Directory for Catholics of the United States* (NCD), approved by the NCCB November 4–17, 1977, approved by the Sacred Congregation for the Clergy, October 30, 1978, published in 1979. • Written for those responsible for catechesis to help catechetical planning and evaluation. It shifted from the narrower focus of the previous conference documents on "educational ministry" and "religious education" to the broader "catechesis" and "catechetical ministry." Chapter 5 expanded the list of principal elements of the Christian message in GCD and BT.
John Paul II, *Catechesi Tradendae*, Apostolic Exhortation on Catechesis in our Time (CT), October 16, 1979. • This papal exhortation motivates the church in its efforts for renewal	

Universal Publications	National Publications, United States

in catechesis. It has a fundamental relationship to evangelization. It is not as strong, however, in its treatment of sacramental and adult catechesis.

John Paul II, *Catechism of the Catholic Church* (CCC), first edition, 1994; second edition, 1997.
  ♦ Not a textbook, but rather intended for those responsible for teaching the people of God. Presented in four parts: the Profession of Faith, the Celebration of the Christian Mystery, Life in Christ, and Christian Prayer.

Congregation for the Clergy, *General Directory for Catechesis* (GDC), August 11, 1997.
  ♦ A reworking of the GCD based on experience and the intervening documents. The list of outstanding elements is replaced by use of the CCC and emphasis on evangelization, gospel message, liturgical catechesis, and inculturation. The baptismal catechumenate "is the model of [the church's] catechizing activity" and "the source of inspiration for post-baptismal catechesis."

United States Conference of Catholic Bishops (USCCB), *Our Hearts Were Burning Within Us: A Pastoral Plan for Adult Faith Formation in the United States* (OHWB), November 17, 1999.
  ♦ Although the US bishops wrote earlier of the importance of total Catholic education, here they stress the primary centrality of adult faith formation. They implored the use of the baptismal catechumenate as an inspiring model.

Universal Publications	National Publications, United States

	• They set out three goals: invite and enable ongoing conversion to Jesus in holiness of life, promote and support active membership in the Christian community, and call and prepare adults to act as disciples in mission to the world.
	
	USCCB, *National Directory for Catechesis* (NDC), approved by the USCCB in June 2003, *recognitio* by the Holy See, published in 2005.
	  • Following the GDC, this also reflects a shift in formational styles and methods. The basic teachings of chapter 5 is replaced with "Catechesis in a Worshiping Community." It stresses the "baptismal catechumenate is the source of inspiration for all catechesis," not just sacramental catechesis. It inspires a gradual nature and approach to catechesis. It is both a process of formation and true school of faith.
	
	USCCB, *United States Catholic Catechism for Adults* (USCCA), approved by the USCCB in November 2004, *recognitio* by the Congregation for the Clergy on November 22, 2005, and for the revision on June 13, 2009, published in 2006 and 2010.
	  • Unlike the CCC, it engages storytelling to begin each chapter with content, then, presented in narrative form. It may also be used directly with adults in their formation.

Pope Francis, *Evangelii Gaudium*, Apostolic Exhortation on the Proclamation of the Gospel in Today's World (EG), November 24, 2013.	

Universal Publications	National Publications, United States

◆ The church must embark on a new era of evangelization as a community of missionary disciples.

Pope Francis, *Gaudete et Exsultate*, Apostolic Exhortation on the Call to Holiness in Today's World (GE), March 19, 2018.
   ◆ Holiness is our path; do not be afraid.
   ◆ Invites us to look to the saint next door.
   ◆ Reflects on the Beatitudes and the works of mercy.

Chapter 5

The Baptismal Catechumenate

Story: Never Knowing It All

My last job before retirement spanned almost thirty years in a diocesan office supporting the work of liturgy and the catechumenate. Every year without fail, in addition to my regular duties and tasks, I got at least one new request—a question or pitch or plea I had never heard.

It kept me on my toes. I knew the basics, but each request drove me to do more reading and research seeking out suitable options for the specific parish or cluster. I concluded early on that my duty to study and learn—and relearn—would never end. The new personnel and new issues required new applications of conventional norms and practices.

Even for a repeated session, perhaps an "old standby," the persons who would be in the room were not the same ones from the last time. Their needs, their input and responses—and the Holy Spirit, and the Word of God, and tradition, and prayer—helped to direct the session and even, at times, change it right in the midst of it.

Praying, Believing, and Living the Christian Life

Life is filled with learning and formation, and relearning and reformation. A teacher continues to read, participates in advanced courses, and works with department members and the entire faculty to further the educational mission. An electrician continues to learn the craft long after the basic journeyman period. Barbers, beauticians, medical technicians, and tax preparers, for example, must meet regular certification requirements. Composers continue to write liturgical songs and choirs continue to add new music to the repertory for the benefit of the assembly whom they support and serve.

Who among us would want a doctor who does not read and study and keep up? Who would want a mechanic who likes the Ford Model A but is not prepared to work on today's more complicated cars?

The same is true for church ministry. Any parish minister who says, "I haven't read a book since I began this ministry" should be embarrassed. Any catechumenal minister who says, "I know all I need to know because I took a class or institute twenty years ago" should also be embarrassed. This is nothing but ecclesial malpractice. Pastors should help them to find something else to do.

I recall my working as a team member with the North American Forum on the Catechumenate flagship Beginnings and Beyond Institute. The team manual to guide presentations was revised five times in those twenty-two years. The ritual book did not change. But our understanding and insights and implementing it did for many, many reasons. We stopped doing some things, we started doing other things because of our own ongoing reflection and formation.

The baptismal catechumenate is at the heart of parish and diocesan ministry. So is evangelization both old and new. So is worship and the liturgy of the church. They are interrelated. They are not in competition. Neither are they fixed, immutable, nor irreformable.

Essentially, the baptismal catechumenate is the formation of unbaptized adults and children of catechetical age (and those baptized in other ecclesial communities whose formation is different from the unbaptized) in a life of discipleship. Conversion to Christ is at the heart of this ministry.

Essentially, evangelization is proclaiming the centrality of Jesus Christ, dead and risen, in our lives, in all lives, in the church and the world. Salvation of all is begun in him and is ongoing still. Faithful proclamation in word and work is at the very heart.

Essentially, liturgy is worship due to God. As the first school of the church, it teaches us what we believe and what we hold dear. It also teaches us how to pray in manifold ways—alone and, most importantly, with others.

All of this has great importance for catechumenal ministry. It is not the task of a few but the task of all the faithful who are baptized into Christ. It is based not on what I personally like, want, or desire. It is rooted in what the whole church—head and members—likes, wants, desires, and needs.

Let us revisit the complaints and expectations in the introduction voiced by some and heard by many and offer suitable ways to address them that are consistent with the vision and norms of the *Rite of Christian Initiation of Adults*.

Seekers Who Say:

- I do not want to/cannot spend a long time at this.
- This must be done before the wedding.
- It will please my (future) in-laws.
- I don't want to do anything in public.

Parish ministers, salaried and volunteer, full-time to very part-time, must remain clear who sets the standard, the norm for sacramental initiation and the Christian life. It is Christ and his church. Not the seeker. Not the one to be initiated.

To Seekers, Ministers Can Say:

- *We don't yet know how long this will take.* This process of conversion to Christ is a manner of careful discernment, regularly done over time. It will take prayerful listening to God by you and us, by you and your family, by your sponsor and godparents, by catechists and pastor. Ultimately, it will take place in the ritual dialogue with the bishop and by him on behalf of the whole church during the Rite of Election at the beginning of some future Lent.

- *Marriage is important*, but so is baptism. We cannot let one formation process rush the other. When you become ready for matrimony, you can marry in the church as a catechumen. Your marriage will become sacramental at your baptism into Christ. We have people here to help you with both of your concerns, both of your needs.

- *Pleased in-laws are a blessing*, but your happiness is the primary concern. So is the life in faith you are exploring and want to live. These are the central questions: What does God have in store for you? What does God want? What do you want? Are you ready now?

- *The Christian life is not private.* Just as we cannot be citizens in private, we cannot be Christian and Catholic in private. We cannot do liturgy in private either, because it is always the public prayer of the church. We will begin slowly and carefully with you, gradually widening the circle to include more of the faith community. We will always protect you and keep you safe. Your sponsor who guides you during formation will also be at your side during public prayer.

Team Members Who Say:

- I will work at this from fall to spring but not in the summer. I need some down time.

- I will come to the sessions when I can, but additional monthly team meetings are not possible.

- I will not/cannot go to workshops or ministry training sessions, either here in the parish or in the region.

- I do not have the RCIA book. I really do not need my own copy of the ritual text. I have not opened the book.

- It is important to keep everyone together, doing the same things at the same time.

- For those who miss a session, we have to provide make-up classes so they can stay on our schedule.

- We have this small group of sponsors to use over and over because they know what to do.

- Our team of ten is now only one or two. I am/we are doing the best I/we can.

To Team Members, the Church Says:

- *Everybody needs down time.* It is a rare business that closes for a month or two or three each year so everyone can go on vacation at the same time. Time away is staggered throughout the year so essential work can continue. Because catechumens may still be in formation (and should not be rushed out of a period unready for what is next), the parish must find ways to stagger vacations and rests so that this necessary work continues. In this way, we always have at least some ministers on the job. In this way, burnout can be avoided.

- *We must be clear about expectations for this core team ministry.* My experience and the experience of many offers this: monthly core team meetings are the first responsibility for members. An hour and a half to two hours is enough for these meetings. They begin and end on time. The meetings are for extended praying and faith sharing (20 to 25 percent of the meeting!), some learning, some review of the sacramental vision, discernment of those in the process, plans and assignments for coming weeks, and any pressing need. This is the gathering no team member misses.

- *Training and formation are ongoing.* I had a pastor—with sound understanding of priesthood, liturgy, and pastoral service—talk with me about his frustration with the catechumenate team. It was quite happy with its limited vision and implementation. The volunteer director did not read diocesan mailings, take part in regional training and meetings, or want to make any modifications suggested by others, the pastor included. Over coffee, we explored options and strategies. Finally, he threw up his hands and said, "I am sort of stuck. I cannot fire a slave. That's what a volunteer director is."

  The church has a wonderful understanding of ecclesial ministry. It is not based on volunteerism. It is rooted in identified need, then discernment of charisms and competencies of persons for attending to what is needed. This requires supervised training and formation. No bishop would say to a man who knocks on the cathedral door asking for priesthood, "Great! Show up next Sunday for ordination."

  A better pastoral approach might be: "I think you have what it takes to do this work. I see these gifts in you [name the gifts]. Here are the expectations. The parish will reimburse you for some or all the needed materials and workshop fees. What do you think?" If the person is unwilling or cannot accept this now, give thanks for the consideration and keep looking, praying, and asking.

- *Using and knowing how to navigate the ritual book is not optional.* The *Rite of Christian Initiation of Adults* is filled with rites, short and long. Pastoral notes are provided for each one to guide good preparation and good celebration. Not only does it provide guidance with norms and options for the full initiation of the unbaptized (RCIA, part I), it also provides related norms and options for the particular circumstances of children (RCIA 252–330; Canada, 242–306), of those with pressing and exceptional needs (RCIA 331–369; Canada, 307–345), of the seriously ill and dying (RCIA 370–399; Canada, 346–375), of the baptized but unformed in the Christian life (RCIA 400–472; Canada, 376–386 and 455–530), and of those baptized and formed in other ecclesial communities (RCIA 473–501; Canada, 387–417). Familiarity with the book makes this clear: one size does not fit all. Regular reading of the ritual text helps us to test and review our parish practice to assure it is consistent with the vision of the rite and suited to those who are now before us.

- *Catechumenal formation is essentially individual pastoral care done within community.* When we do regular discernment, we are aware of current needs and realities. When the baptismal catechumenate is ongoing and year-round, we will always have "senior" and "junior" catechumens in process—some ready for this coming Lent and Easter, some not. The group, then, is not a fixed class from which everyone graduates at the same time. It is a temporary group that mirrors the parish assembly with people "all over the place," at various stages and needs on this journey of faith. Although we are all in this together, we are not all at the same place at the same time. *Their* schedule is of the utmost importance. It is more important than any fixed and rigid course outline pulled from the file cabinet.

- *Who is missing what?* If we believe that Christ is present and living among us and that the Holy Spirit guides our lives, then each of us and all of us are right where we need to be. We trust grace. Each catechumen truly has his or her own schedule that endeavors to mesh with church life. Work duties, family obligations, and life dictate this. Long-haul truckers and railroad engineers, for example, may be away for seven to ten days at a time. When the parish engages in regular discernment, caring for individual needs as well as the vision of the rite, it discovers they did not "miss" anything. Their formation may just take longer by attending to what they are able to do and in ways they can be done. The same is true for those who just do not show up with regularity. Discernment helps us plumb the reasons (RCIA 1, 37, 42–43, 76, 120–21; Canada, 1, 37, 42–43, 76, 107–8)—and then responsibly respond.

- *Sponsors.* Because the baptismal catechumenate is the task of all the baptized (RCIA 4 and 9), the parish staff and team must continually seek ways to help the faithful do their job. Sponsors have a critical role. I suggest this: Ask a parishioner only one time to be a sponsor. It is hard and long and weekly work when done correctly. If the match up was carefully done, the sponsor may be asked by the catechumen to take on the permanent role of godparent. Therefore, the parish must continually look for, ask, and prepare new sponsors. A pool of sponsors allows the parish to make suitable matches in timely ways.

- *Doing the best.* Every time I have talked with persons who have become a one- or two-person catechumenate team, they expressed frustration and regret. They instinctively know one or two people is not enough. They are often unsure or unsuccessful in securing more help. *Our Hearts Were Burning Within Us* recommends three to ten members for such an important core team to oversee such important work (pp. 48–50). Members should not be created in the image or likeness of the director. The team needs to be a diverse group—like-minded on the vision presented by the baptismal catechumenate—but varied in charisms, temperament, age, and life experience.

  Pastors are fairly astute. They ask an active person to take on an additional task because there is evidence for another job well done. Parishioners are fairly astute, too. They know that when asked to do a certain job, they will likely have it for life. Death may be the only way out. What if the pastor says: You are the person to be part of the catechumenate team because of these gifts and charisms; what if person X takes over what you are now doing, so you are freer to do this new work? We will reassess this every year (or two).

Pastors and Staff Members Who Say:

- I have a lot of other things to do. I need to be more efficient with this one ministry among many others.

- I know how to do this with a sixteen to twenty-week teaching plan that has been used over and over. I know it works. It gives them what they need.

- We can catch up on missed classes during Lent even after the Rite of Election.

- Because lay parishioners do not have a thorough academic training, I will do all or most of the teaching.

- You, Deacon, because of your academic formation and degree, have everything you need to be in charge of the RCIA. You do not need additional formation. You do not need a big team.

- The church only gives us an ideal. It is okay if we do not achieve it.

- The diocese only makes this work more difficult.

To Pastors and Staff Members, the Church Says:

- *Busy priests.* The parish of my childhood in the 1950s had nine Benedictine sisters in the school and three priests in the rectory. This is not true today. In a city that is now double in size, the school with no sisters is now shared with the new neighboring parish, and the rectory has one priest. Pastors do have a lot to oversee, but gone are the days when they did everything. Just as the priest cannot responsibly do liturgy all by himself or by cutting corners, neither can he do so with the catechumenate. He can discern the essential elements in which he can and must engage while engaging others in this parish-wide ministry. Review the necessary list of ministers in the Introduction of the ritual text (RCIA 4 and 9–16).

- *RCIA is not a short course.* Priests know that preaching and celebrating sacraments are essential work. They take prayer and reflection, diligence and time. Except for vacation, it all occurs every week. The unfolding of the mystery of Christ for and with the faithful occurs over the entire liturgical year, and the same is true for catechumenal formation. This conformation to Christ cannot be shoe-horned into a sixteen to twenty-week course that is more information delivery than transformational conversion and discipleship discovery. The agenda found in the Lectionary and the Missal, the liturgical year and special rites that shape the already baptized, is the same agenda for catechumens used in suitably initiatory ways.

- *The true character of Lent.* The Forty Days of Lent is already filled with election, three scrutinies, two presentations as well as all the other special Lenten praying, fasting, giving, and doing. Each requires necessary preparation and suitable reflection afterward. Attempting to add in missing topics of the previous period shortchanges Lent. What the bishop asks and declares during the Rite of Election (RCIA 131; Canada, 118) must be dealt with in appropriate ways before coming to the cathedral church for that declaration done in prayer. Nothing can stand in the way, nothing in the suitable initiatory formation can be incomplete.

- *Trust and prepare the faithful.* Much of pastoral ministry is never ending. One of the reasons priests valued the old style convert instruction in pre-Vatican II days was the experience of a pastoral task with a clear beginning and end. Many found it hard to give up in the 1970s and 1980s. Some still find that method hard to abandon. Catechumenal formation is not a single-person ministry. Academic theology degree work is a blessing but does not adequately prepare a person for the diversity of adult learning styles needed for faith formation. Dioceses do provide catechetical and lay ecclesial ministry formation. Neighboring dioceses do as well. So do regional onsite and online sessions. See to the preparation of parishioners to do some and not all of this formation. Expend parish funds to help this happen.

- *Ideal or norm.* The Gospel of Matthew enjoins us to be perfect as God is perfect (Matt 5:48). It is another way of embracing the golden rule—love God and love neighbor as I love myself. This is normative for Christian life. We know we fall short. That is why Lent is an annual occurrence. That is why we celebrate the reconciling gift of penance. That is why most Masses include a Penitential Act as part of the Introductory Rites.

That is why we feed on Christ Sunday after Sunday. Mere ideals let us off the hook because they are so big, so out there, so unachievable. Norms do not. Because the baptismal catechumenate is normative, we have duties and responsibilities to strive toward and incrementally work toward that "perfection." We cannot just make things up for celebrating Mass, and the same is true for this initiatory catechesis and formation. Diocesan staffers can help the parish to set reasonable short and long-term goals and strategies that embrace this vision.

- *Diocesan staffers are your advocates and friends.* Occasionally, diocesan staffers do have to tell parish ministers what must be done. But, most often, they offer options and methods suited to the parish. I was three months into new diocesan work after nine years of parish ministry overseeing liturgy and the catechumenate. During the celebration of Christmas Midnight Mass that was essentially poorly celebrated, lazy liturgy, I had this insight. Because I no longer have the same control to affect good parish liturgy throughout the diocese as I did when I worked in a single parish, I needed a new approach. Now as a diocesan staffer, when requests are made or questions asked, I provide three to seven possibilities (nice Trinitarian and sacramental numbers). One may be clearly wrong or not suitable, but, though possible, there is an option that is easy to cross off. With the rest, my task was to list the strengths and weaknesses for this parish's implementation. The many staffers in many dioceses take a similar approach. When at their best, they want parishes and its ministers to work smart, to stay within the broad boundaries of liturgical adaptation, and to be faithful.

Values for the Baptismal Catechumenate

The preceding chapters make the case that the formation of catechumens is not radically different than the ongoing formation of the faithful. It is initiatory in focus, true. It never attempts,

however, to be complete. That is the task of postbaptismal catechesis, the task of mystagogy, the task of a lifetime.

But there are certain values to which we must attend as normative dimensions of Christian initiation. There could be twelve,
there could be four. Here are seven that help us to remember essential elements and behaviors that leave room for the action of
the Holy Spirit.

Paschal Mystery

From the very beginning before time began, God chose to love
us. God spoke and created all things good. God spoke again and
human beings came into being, made very good. In time, God
became human, like us in all things but sin, not as correction but
out of a desire to love us all.

Jesus Christ is a manifestation of that intense love. He lived,
suffered, died, is living still, and is present among us in manifold
ways. This is his paschal mystery. Because of what happened to
him, all are saved, all redeemed. It is important to us because we
believe what happened to him happens to us. Our salvation by
this dead and risen Christ provides the pattern for our dying and
rising in big and little ways and all ways in between. None are
the end of us. At every death, we are raised up to life renewed, to
life anew, even at the falling apart of our bodies at the end of this
life as we know it.

This way of being is at the heart of the baptismal catechumenate
because it is at the heart of Christian living. The whole of the
Christian life is to act and think like Christ, the one whose name
we bear. Each Easter Vigil we hear proclaimed the mystagogical
reflection on baptism from Romans 6:

> Are you unaware that we who have been baptized into Christ
> Jesus were baptized into his death? We were indeed buried with
> him through baptism into death, so that, just as Christ was raised
> from the dead by the glory of the Father, we too might live in
> newness of life.

This requires conversion to him in a radical way of living, transformed in him to a life focused not on self, conformed to him in all things.

Parish Context

Elected officials, even during national elections, will say: "All politics is local." Our experience of church is essentially the same. Without negating our belonging to the universal church, we use "local church" to mean the diocese. Just as each diocese is interrelated to all dioceses of the whole Catholic Church, a single parish does not stand alone. It is connected to the other parishes forming the diocese, the local church.

But church is fundamentally lived at the parish level. It is lived in the neighborhood and town. A parish can exist because it has the personnel and resources to function—enabled to celebrate liturgy and sacraments, provide requisite pastoral care for the faithful, and care for human needs of parishioners and non-parishioners alike. That is why the baptismal catechumenate is parish based. The National Statutes for the Catechumenate (USA) make this clear:

> If the catechumenal preparation takes place in a non-parochial setting such as a center, school, or other institution, the catechumens should be introduced into the Christian life of a parish or similar community from the very beginning of the catechumenate, so that after their initiation and mystagogy they will not find themselves isolated from the ordinary life of the Christian people. (4)

That is also why catechumenal pastoral care expects and requires all the baptized to assist in this work (RCIA 4 and 9). We become more holy through the help of the saint next door. We become more holy in the gatherings of the saints Sunday after Sunday. We become more holy in working alongside the saints throughout the week off the parish campus.

Apprenticeship

It is possible for someone to come to belief in God without the help of others, but no one can become Christian alone. Christians believe that because God is triune, Christian life is also communal. We learn this from Jesus's own behavior while he walked this earth. He lived with apostles, with disciples, with followers, and with crowds. He interacted with believers and nonbelievers alike.

Those who followed him did so because they hung around with him. After his ascension into heaven, those who followed did so because they hung around with original followers. Followers follow followers down to this very day.

The process of Christian initiation is not a one-and-done proposition as is learning to tie shoelaces. Once that skill is mastered, it is done automatically, rarely requiring a refresher course. The baptismal catechumenate is more like finding the right pair of shoes and breaking them in so that they are comfortable for the task. One pair cannot last a lifetime.

Ad Gentes, the Second Vatican Council's Decree on the Church's Missionary Activity, declares that the catechumenate

> is not merely an exposition of dogmatic truths and norms of morality, but a period of formation in the entire christian life, an apprenticeship of suitable duration, during which the disciples will be joined to Christ their teacher. (14)

As with every apprenticeship in craft or skill or art, information delivery has an important place. It cannot, however, be the only or even the primary method of formation. There is learning by observation, by practice, by doing and redoing again—and again.

That is the behavior to which the period of the catechumenate, the time between Acceptance and Election, is devoted: the fourfold training and formation of catechesis, community, liturgy and prayer, and the service of apostolic life (RCIA 75 and 78).

Liturgy

There is the ancient saying *lex orandi, lex credendi* that is credited to Prosper of Aquitaine (d. 460). It is literally translated: the rule or law of prayer is the rule of belief. It means that prayer shapes belief; in our praying, we come to believe; doctrine develops and follows upon liturgy.

Catechism of the Catholic Church

The Church's faith precedes the faith of the believer who is invited to adhere to it. When the Church celebrates the sacraments, she confesses the faith received from the apostles— whence the ancient saying: *lex orandi, lex credendi* (or: *legem credendi lex statuat supplicandi,* according to Prosper of Aquitaine [5th cent.]). The law of prayer is the law of faith: the Church believes as she prays. Liturgy is a constitutive element of the holy and living Tradition. (1124)

Thus, we can say in confidence, liturgy is the first school of the church. It is a school rich in imagery and word, symbol and action, silence and song, preaching and prayer. It is not a school of exams or graduations. Liturgy is first and foremost the action of Christ. Liturgy is also the action of the people of God doing God's work. We do it because it is our desire and our need.

That is why not only clergy need familiarity with all the rites in the *Rite of Christian Initiation of Adults.* All the special ministers need to know them in their bones and in their hearts as well. Look at the Rite of Acceptance as an example to make this point. Simply put, this rite is the nexus between basic seeking and initial conversion to Christ that begins the weekly training and formation of a more complete, though initiatory, conformation to that same Christ. But the rite gives us much more about the completion of the period of inquiry and the focus and guide to the following period.

- Inquirers gather outside the church building because they are seeking something of which they are not yet a part.

- Sponsors gather with them because no one enters this Christic journey alone.

- The faithful come out to surround them in support and prayer.

- The celebrant, on behalf of the church, greets them as friends. This is not a first meeting.

- Before any questioning, all may sing of an ardent longing for God. Psalm 63 is suggested, which is also a premier psalm for Morning Prayer: "Oh God, you are my God, for you I long."

- Dialogue follows, ritually confirming the mutual discernment that brought the first period of evangelization and precatechumenate to a close.

- Based on this actual dialogue, the celebrant elicits a first acceptance of the Gospel. Although three texts are provided of about a hundred words each, the rubric reads: "The celebrant addresses the candidates [for this rite], adapting one of the following formularies or similar words to the answers received in the opening dialogue" (52). He does not read the printed words! Instead, the one who presides uses the prior discernment, conversations with sponsors and team, and the actual opening dialogue to plumb their desire to follow Christ, to be his disciple, to live the Christian life, ending with something like: are you prepared for this journey, are you ready to live this life, are you willing to accept?

- The sponsors and assembly formally affirm the candidates' "yes" and pledge their help and then acclaim the praise of God in song.

- Only then are all the senses signed with the cross for Christ to take hold of all they think, hear, see, speak, hold dear, and do. In this signing, the seekers take on the new identity and name of catechumens.

- They are invited by name to come into the church building to share with the faithful at the table of God's word. In crossing that threshold, in entering through the doorway, those who were outsiders are now insiders. Standing within the order of catechumens, they are members of the household of Christ. Something new is happening.

- All enter singing about the import of listening to God, about tasting God's goodness.

- The Liturgy of the Word begins with a brief instruction to the catechumens and to all. It is to focus our attention on the dignity of God's word proclaimed and heard in the church building by the church. Once again, no text is provided. To help his preparation, the one who presides may recall the words of the bishop at the beginning of the very first Liturgy of the Word in a church about to be dedicated:

  > May the word of God
  >   resound always in this building,
  > to open for you the mystery of Christ
  > and to bring about your salvation in the Church.

- If it is a weekday, readings are chosen "that are suited to the new catechumens." The provided Lectionary texts are the call of Abram and Sarai and the call of the first disciples. If celebrated within the parish Sunday Mass, look for a Sunday with suitable readings that deal with following the Lord, taking up the cross, leaving something behind, discipleship, living in the kingdom of God.

- The homily does what all good homilies do: it takes into account the mystery being celebrated and the needs of catechumens and faithful in the assembly.

- Intercessions specifically for the catechumens follow concluding with a prayer over them.

- Then they are dismissed to reflect more deeply on the Word of God just heard while the faithful usually remain for the Liturgy of the Eucharist.

This ritual activity shapes the period that follows and launches the catechumens and the church into a rich formation of discipleship, the spoken and living Word of God, and Sunday centered on the paschal mystery of the ever-present Christ Jesus.

Attention to the prayers and rubrics gives us necessary information and a richer grasp of what we are to do. Liturgy knowingly and richly celebrated, liturgy done well, deepens our faith and shapes our belief. This is hard work.

United States Conference of Catholic Bishops,
Sing to the Lord: Music in Divine Worship
Faith grows when it is well expressed in celebration. Good celebrations can foster and nourish faith. Poor celebrations may weaken it. (5)

Using Symbol

"A picture is worth a thousand words." As wordy as the church's prayer can be, it is also rich in symbol use, fluent in signs that often speak wordlessly. Symbols are the matter of sacramental action—water, light, ritual clothing, oil, bread and wine, laying on of hands, blessing and exchanging rings, the sign of the cross. To this list, we add the Word of God, ministerial action, liturgical music, and the assembly, as well as the altar, ambo, chair, font, images of holy ones, and holy action. Seasonally, we add wreaths, trees, crèches, candles, and colors. Beauty helps us to peer into the wonderful mystery of God.

Using symbols in big ways helps to reflect big realities. No one would attempt to bury the dead with three teaspoons of dirt. Although three teaspoons of water are valid matter for baptism, three generous pourings or three breath-gasping plunges beneath the water reflect the baptismal dying and rising to new life in Christ in a richer way. A host large enough to be seen by those in the last pew during the elevations within the eucharistic prayer reflects the One who is our food in a richer, clearer way.

Large signs of the cross made by priest and sponsors during the signing of the senses during Rite of Acceptance reflect our desire for Christ to be present in everything the catechumens will touch, taste, see, hear, and feel.

Sponsors who guide catechumens by the hand or arm throughout special prayers for them and assemblies who physically surround them for prayer loudly speak that catechumens do not stand alone. They are part of a caring and protective assembly of believers.

Key symbols used in big ways help to reflect big realities. There is the living Word of God, who is Christ present among us in many ways. There are sacraments that unite us to the church, head and members.

Sacramental Readiness

Parents and grandparents are thrilled at what they observe. The child first feeds on breast milk, then takes and holds a bottle, then takes pureed food on a spoon, then takes finger food. In a while, after some experimentation, bowls, cups, utensils come into play. The child also rolls over and sits up, grasps and holds, crawls and walks when ready. There is no set week or month when every new child does the same thing. They learn by doing. They learn by watching, by coaching, by trying—and trying again. A child crawls when he is ready. A child walks when she is ready.

Sacraments are celebrated when readiness is established—not before, not after. The baptismal catechumenate sets out times throughout the process to discern readiness.

Sacramental readiness is determined bit-by-bit, gradually over time. It is discernment that is cooperative between the individual and the church. In the case of unbaptized persons, every period and every liturgy sets out needs, requirements, and judgments. The summary at the very beginning of the ritual text stresses mystery, proclamation, freedom, covenant, conversion, spirituality, and timing (RCIA 1). The details for evangelization and precatechumenate imply noting changes in behavior (RCIA 37–38). Readiness for acceptance demands certain "evidence" of prerequisites, "evaluation" and "judging" of motives and dispositions (RCIA 42–43). The catechumenate period seeks Christian maturity by means of the fourfold pastoral formation and training (RCIA 75).

Nothing is determined *a priori*, that is, based on theory rather than experience (RCIA 76). Election expects certain observable behaviors that are clearly named within the rite itself prior to celebration (RCIA 120–21 and 131; Canada, 107–8 and 118).

In the case of unbaptized children of catechetical age, permission, age appropriate formation extended over several years, companions, and suitable celebrations all play a role (RCIA 252–59; Canada, 242–49). In the case of baptized but uncatechized Christians, discernment is required to establish how much training and formation is needed (RCIA 400–410; Canada, 376–86 and 455–62). In the case of a formed Christian of a separated ecclesial community, no greater burden than necessary is placed in the way of unity at the table of the Lord (RCIA 473; Canada, 387).

Attention to readiness assures that sacramental life can be embraced and lived. Attention to readiness prevents rushing someone forward because some plan says it happens now. Attention to readiness prevents us from having someone take the next step simply because others are taking it now. Attention to readiness prevents holding persons hostage to a schedule or calendar when, in fact, they are ready now.

Liturgical Catechesis and Mystagogical Catechesis

Of all the styles of learning and formation in faith, liturgical and mystagogical catechesis are paramount within the baptismal catechumenate. Just as attention to Sunday and all of liturgy shaped the church from its earliest days and thus shaped the formation of doctrine, this first school of the church still shapes us today. It does so every week. It is this expression of faith in Christ that tells us who we are and whose we are.

But as important as liturgical catechesis is, I am becoming more and more sure that mystagogical catechesis needs an ever-increasing prominence in church life, in preaching, in every catechetical endeavor, and, thus, in the ministry of the baptismal catechumenate. Mystagogy is not just for Easter Time. We need to do it in little and big ways all year long.

Although many agree with this, it is my experience that far fewer have the art, the skill, and the patience to do it effectively. It requires intimate knowledge of the church's rites, a knowing in the bones. It requires an understanding of the theological implications of these rites. It requires attention to human experience as well as to art, the senses, and poetic language. Although there is some helpful writing on this, we need, I think, much more help on methodology to form mystagogues in the skill and art of effective mystagogy.

Let us hope and pray for more intensive work in this area.

Kathleen Hughes, RSCJ, *Becoming the Sign: Sacramental Living in a Post-Conciliar Church*

I believe we need a new effort, not of liturgical *catechesis* but of liturgical *mystagogy*—a word used to describe the opening up of the mysteries for believers through reflection on actual experience. The early church made an important distinction between these two forms of teaching . . . Mystagogy . . . generally took place *after* the experience of the sacraments of initiation and was more about helping the newly initiated go deeper into the mysteries that had been celebrated at the Easter Vigil. . . .

What if we found ways of revisiting our sacramental experience, engaging in a holy remembering of the event, the words, the gestures, the objects, the sights, the scents, the music and the silence? What if mystagogy became our bridge between experience and celebration? . . .

This would be a new kind of liturgical formation, made up more of poetry than of prose, and it could be for the remaking of our sacramental experience if we let it work its way into our minds and hearts. (Mahwah, NJ: Paulist Press, 2013, pp. 77–79)

Helpful Resources

Roman Ritual: Rite of Christian Initiation of Adults

Ritual Edition—hardbound with ribbons for use during liturgy. Study Edition—softbound with the same text for highlighting and making notes.

English edition for use in the dioceses of the United States of America, 1988. Several publishers.

Spanish edition, *Rito de la Iniciación Cristiana de Adultos,* for use in the dioceses of the United States of America, 1991.

Edition for use in the dioceses of Canada, 1987.

Every team member needs a personal copy.

About Aspects of the Baptismal Catechumenate

Leisa Anslinger. *A Vision for Conversion: Eight Steps to Radically Change Your RCIA Process.* Collegeville, MN: Liturgical Press, 2019.

> Walks you through the eight most effective ways to move your parish RCIA process from maintenance mode into a true conversion journey that inspires seekers to lifelong discipleship.

Mary Birmingham. *Year-Round Catechumenate.* Chicago: Liturgy Training Publications, 2002.

> Offers practical ways to grasp the vision and process that exists at the heart of the church's life and on the same schedule as the church: every day, all year long.

Michael Clay. *A Harvest for God: Christian Initiation in the Rural and Small-Town Parish.* Chicago: Liturgy Training Publications, 2003.

> Provides templates and methods for session design in each period and for major celebrations.

Michael E. Connors, CSC. *Preaching for Discipleship: Preparing Homilies for Christian Initiation.* Chicago: Liturgy Training Publications, 2018.

> Includes tips, suggestions, and sample homilies with comments for preaching to all the faithful during initiation rites and throughout the year.

John Huels. *The Catechumenate and the Law: A Pastoral and Canonical Commentary for the Church in the United States.* Chicago: Liturgy Training Publications, 1994.

> A basic primer on rights and duties, requirements and options.

Ronald Lewinski. *Guide for Sponsors.* Fourth edition. Chicago: Liturgy Training Publications, 2008.

> Helps the formation of sponsors and godparents and is a useful reference for them in this ministry.

Ronald Lewinski. *An Introduction to the RCIA: The Vision of Christian Initiation.* Chicago: Liturgy Training Publications, 2018.

> A basic book, suitable for team formation. Provides an overview of the four stages of initiation and their accompanying rituals. Gives questions for reflection and discussion.

Diana Macalintal. *Your Parish* Is *the Curriculum: RCIA in the Midst of the Community.* Collegeville, MN: Liturgical Press, 2018.

> Helps ministers to focus on what is already present in parish life and necessary for initiation ministry.

Michael H. Marchal. *The Spirit at Work: Conversion and the RCIA.* Franklin Park, IL: World Library Publications, 2010.

> Addresses basic and foundational issues for this ministry: conversions, discernment, Eucharist, candidates, and the initiating community. The core team could use it in the study portion of meetings to focus on the vision of the catechumenate.

Thomas H. Morris. *The RCIA: Transforming the Church; A Resource for Pastoral Implementation.* Revised and updated edition. New York: Paulist Press, 1997.

> Especially helpful for the director. Covers the whole process. Offers suggestions and options rather than only one way to do something.

Ron A. Oakham, editor. *One at the Table: The Reception of Baptized Christians.* Chicago: Liturgy Training Publications, 1995.

> Part I is most helpful on vision and methods for bringing baptized Christians into the full communion of the Catholic Church.

Timothy P. O'Malley. *Divine Blessing: Liturgical Formation in the RCIA.* Collegeville, MN: Liturgical Press, 2019.

> Shows us how we can break out of a classroom model *about* liturgy and instead invite seekers to be formed by the risen Christ *through* the liturgy.

Rita Burns Senseman. *A Child's Journey: The Christian Initiation of Children.* San Jose, CA: TeamRCIA, 1998.

> Provides solid, practical advice on the vision and needs for the special adaptations for children. Covers each of the periods and provides guidance for discernment.

Rita Burns Senseman, Victoria Tufano, Paul Turner. *Guide for Celebrating Christian Initiation with Children.* Chicago: Liturgy Training Publications, 2016.

> Provides theological and historical overview, practical advice, Q&A, suitable catechesis, and liturgy with children.

Donna Steffen, SC. *Discernment in Christian Initiation.* Chicago: Liturgy Training Publications, 2018.

> Revises the previous editions of her book *Discerning Disciples: Listening for God's Voice in Christian Initiation.* Describes the decision-making process; serves to improve listening skills; helps to ask the right questions at the right time. The appendix contains specific suggestions for interviews during the four stages of the catechumenate and offers a format for a discernment day before the Rite of Election.

Victoria Tufano, Paul Turner, D. Todd Williamson. *Guide for Celebrating Christian Initiation with Adults.* Chicago: Liturgy Training Publications, 2016.

> Provides theological and historical overview, practical advice, step-by-step guide for formation.

Paul Turner. *Celebrating Initiation: A Guide for Priests.* Franklin Park, IL: World Library Publications, 2007.

> Leads priests through twenty-six rites of initiation, including all the various rites of the RCIA, adaptations for already baptized candidates, and so on. Practical advice on reading the notes and celebrating the rites.

Paul Turner. *Q&A on the RCIA: A Guide to Understanding Christian Initiation.* Chicago: Liturgy Training Publications, 2019.

> Provides short answers to over a hundred frequently asked questions. All questions are part of the table of contents, making the book easy to use. Divided into six parts: Groundwork Questions, Pre-Catechumenate, Catechumenate, Purification and Enlightenment, Initiation, and Mystagogy.

Paul Turner. *When Other Christians Become Catholic*. Collegeville, MN: Liturgical Press, 2007.

> With historical and ecumenically sensitive analysis, helps ministers to think more carefully about the baptismal unity of Christians.

Nick Wagner. *Field Hospital Catechesis: The Core Content for RCIA Formation*. Collegeville, MN: Liturgical Press, 2018.

> Explores the nine core teachings of the church that make up this first proclamation (*kerygma*). Readers will become catechists and evangelists equipped to bring healing to those around them.

Nick Wagner. *Seek the Living God: Five RCIA Inquiry Questions for Making Disciples*. Collegeville, MN: Liturgical Press, 2017.

> Provides an individualized formation path for each inquirer, leading them to lifelong discipleship.

Nick Wagner. *The Way of Faith: A Field Guide for the RCIA Process*. New London, CT: Twenty-Third Publications, 2008.

> A practical guide for leaders and team members.

Nick Wagner and Diana Macalintal. TeamRCIA website: www.TeamRCIA.com.

> Articles, bookstore, ask questions of lead authors.

Stephen S. Wilbricht, CSC. *The Role of the Priest in Christian Initiation*. Chicago: Liturgy Training Publications, 2017.

> Guides priests through the periods and steps, highlights the vision of the rite, and addresses their role as a shepherd and guide. A glossary and index are included.

Part II.
Steps for Preparing a Week during the Period of the Catechumenate

Part I, Forming the Faithful in Christ, addressed the many ways that the baptized encountered the dead and risen Christ Jesus in past ages and still encounter him this day. Key among these ways are:

- engaging in paschal mystery, that is, sharing in Christ's redemptive dying and rising day by day;

- participating in Sunday as well as the whole of the liturgical year, week after week and year after year;

- and attending to the ongoing need for a catechetical formation through one's entire life that is much more comprehensive than mere religious instruction.

Although initiatory or basic catechesis describes the ways the church trains and forms the unbaptized, this catechumenal formation is not separate from the wholistic catechetical plan of the church. (Nor are the steps we take for the formation of the many baptized candidates who may also be in our care.) We shape catechumens best when we share with them—in initiatory ways—what we believe, cherish, and know. We do this best Sunday by Sunday and season by season. We treat them as the apprentices they are by:

- reading Scripture with them and hearing the spoken Word of God, Christ himself, proclaimed in the assembly and broken open in preaching, song, and prayer;

- living alongside them the communal life that Christians embrace;

- standing shoulder to shoulder with them in prayer and daily life;

- and working together with them at mercy works and justice tasks.

We treat them—in initiatory ways—as ones transformed by Jesus Christ and conformed to him.

There is a seismic shift in catechumenal formation resulting from the reforms of the Second Vatican Council. *Father Smith Instructs Jackson* by Archbishop John Noll, published in 1913, presented a method common in that preconciliar era. It was most often structured classes, one-on-one in delivery, focused on giving central information about the faith. There are newer works in print that still follow that pattern—information delivery apart from the agenda of Sunday found in Lectionary, Missal, and liturgical song. I do not recommend any of them.

Let me address these two competing styles in more detail. The nine-month catechism approach provides a syllabus (an outline of the topics in a course of study) of the items that will be taught. It usually follows a hierarchy of beliefs, an order beginning with God and ending with the last things of death, end of the world, and judgment. Popular catechisms are usually organized this way. Look at the Nicene Creed; it is also organized in this manner. Note, however, that like the Lord's Prayer, the Creed, expressing the heart of the church's faith, is ritually presented to the elect during Lent after the period of the catechumenate is complete. The Rite of Election has been celebrated and initiation during the Easter Vigil is three weeks away.

Catechumenal catechists, and all those involved in any catechetical effort, I argue, cannot rely solely on preset lesson plans such as these. They may deliver important information about the faith, but, by themselves alone, they cannot engender faithful relationship with Jesus Christ and his church. The basic ongoing formation of Christians and, thus, of catechumens, follows a different syllabus: the liturgical year. It has a specific booklist: Lectionary, Missal, liturgical song book as well as other rites and prayers. It covers all the essential beliefs but in an organization that dances up and down the hierarchy list, usually covering topics more than once.

Better are plans and methods that let us design a training and formation endeavor suited to the Sunday texts, the essentials of Christian life, and the catechumens who stand and sit with us right now. Here are some authors with worthy methods:

- Michael Clay. *A Harvest for God: Christian Initiation in the Rural and Small-Town Parish*. Chicago: Liturgy Training Publications, 2003.

- Thomas H. Groome. *Sharing Faith: A Comprehensive Approach to Religious Education and Pastoral Ministry—The Way of Shared Praxis*. New York: HarperSanFrancisco, 1991.

- Gilbert Ostdiek. *Catechesis for Liturgy: A Program for Parish Involvement*. Portland, OR: OCP, 1986.

- Joe Paprocki. *Beyond the Catechist's Toolbox: Catechesis That Not Only Informs but Also Transforms*. Chicago: Loyola Press, 2013.

I am more and more convinced that good catechesis and good preaching work together. Good preachers and good catechists are good colleagues and friends. Here, in part II, is a method of eight steps with annotated bibliography that builds on that conviction and will help the parish catechumenate team to achieve a training and pastoral formation that is faithful to the fourfold plan of RCIA 75.

Here are the steps for Preparing a Week during the Period of the Catechumenate:

1. Praying with the Liturgical Texts

2. Consulting with Some Liturgical Ministers

3. Consulting with Past and Present and Future Weeks

4. Drafting a Suitable Focus

5. Uncovering the Meaning of the Texts

6. Redrafting the Focus

7. Designing the Week

8. Sharing the Design

Note the order of these steps. It helps to fight the urge to begin with "What will I teach this week? What will I say?" Before asking that question, we must ask (and then listen), "What is Christ saying?"

The steps may seem daunting, even overwhelming at first. But this logical ordering can prevent wasted time. Once the steps become familiar, steps 1 through 4 can take about one hour. The last four steps may take about another two or three. When I took the educational semester in college (I thought I wanted to teach high school history), the rule of thumb was three to four preparation hours for every teaching hour. When I took homiletics in graduate school, the rule of thumb was ten preparation hours for a ten-minute homily or twenty hours for a five-minute one. We learned it only took five hours to preach twenty minutes. It takes more time to winnow all the possible information into a concise, cogent, and clear event for the listening ear.

With fourteen years' experience of implementing the *Rite of Christian Initiation of Adults*, the US bishops issued a clear directive concerning the length of formation in this second period: at least one year for formation if not more. National Statute 6 is "particular law" for all the dioceses of the United States and is consistent with the norms of the ritual text. It trusts the year-round approach over a merely academic year. It trusts the agenda of Sunday and the liturgical year over a shorter list of favored topics. It trusts discernment of sacramental readiness for each catechumen over everyone doing everything at the same time.

Step 1

Praying with the Liturgical Texts

Story: Preparing for Sunday

As a full-time parish staff member, I worked with liturgy and the fledgling baptismal catechumenate from 1975 to 1984. It was not until 1991, however, as a mere parishioner and volunteer on the catechumenate team while doing diocesan ministry, that I fell into a regular plan of praying with the Sunday Mass texts every week.

After some consternation, complaints, and concerns, the parish made the jump from a nine-month RCIA schedule, which was fairly consistent from year to year, to a year-round approach for doing catechumenal ministry. In any given month, I was either a dismissal minister or primary catechist for one Sunday. This assignment led me to spend time with Lectionary *and* Missal texts each week. This weekly work helped to put the assigned Sunday in context with what preceded and followed. Mere reading led to praying. Praying led to an enriched connection to the liturgical year that moved beyond my academic knowledge to one of deeper awareness and insight into God's saving activity.

Praying to Discern God's Active Presence

Because Sunday and the liturgical year is so important to a living faith embedded in the paschal mystery of Jesus Christ, the church wants ministers and faithful alike to attend to certain things concerning Mass. They are:

- the assigned Bible readings of the *Lectionary for Mass*;

- the assigned prayers of the *Roman Missal*, plus any additions from the *Book of Blessings* or sacramental ritual book;

- and the liturgical season and the specific feast.

That is why the very first thing that catechumenal ministers need to do in preparing for a week in the period of the catechumenate, just as every preacher and liturgical music director does, is first pray with all the principal texts of the Sunday. I suggest this as a regular and weekly task, even if you have no assigned ministry duty in that week.

The Scripture readings are first in our attention because the prayers and the music are often written in that biblical language and imagery. In them, when proclaimed in the assembly, Christ speaks. He speaks not just long ago but today. Beginning with them will inform our understanding, appreciation, and, on occasion, our choice of the other texts.

St. Jerome, from the prologue of the commentary on Isaiah

Where there is ignorance of Scripture there is ignorance of Christ. (*Liturgy of the Hours*, Office of Readings, September 30)

Start with the appointed Bible readings in the *Lectionary for Mass*. Move beyond mere reading. Begin with the gospel, for it sets the tone for the series, then move to the first reading, then the psalm, and then the second reading. During the major seasons of Advent,

Christmas, Lent, and Easter, all the readings have the same focus and are in harmony, as it were, with each other. During Ordinary Time, however, all but the second reading have the same focus.

After the Lectionary readings, pray with the texts of the *Roman Missal*, at least those of the Introductory Rites. Finally, pray with any special or seasonal rite, such as the blessing of a wreath, crèche, ashes, persons, and the like. This awareness of the liturgical season and feast also sets a context for the Sunday and thus for our praying.

The praying at this step 1 is personal at first. It gives time and space to wrestle with what God and Christ may be saying to you. Only then can application be made to others in the church and the world.

Some Methods for Praying with Sunday Texts

This step calls for more than a cursory reading of the Sunday texts. Time is needed for consciously being in the presence of God. One method is *lectio divina* (divine reading) with the steps of Read, Ponder, Pray, and Contemplate. Another is Ignatian contemplation, which uses the senses to place oneself within the reading. Still another is to dwell on words or phrases that stand out and ask, "What might God be saying?" Consider, even if only occasionally, a small faith sharing group. *Fulfilled in Your Hearing*, by the US bishops, offers a sixty-five-minute method (see details in step 2 below). There are other ways. You can even make up your own. You do not have to stick with one method.

Necessary Resources

Each person involved in catechumenal catechesis, that is, the formation during the period of the catechumenate, needs easy access to the following. The parish makes a worthy investment when it buys these basic books for the members of the baptismal catechumenate team. In some dioceses, they may be offered at discount.

Lectionary for Mass, Sunday Volume

Free access to the readings:

USA, using the New American Bible, Revised Edition (NABRE): www .usccb.org/bible.

Canada, using the New Revised Standard Version (NRSV): www.cccb.ca.

Study (paperback) editions:

USA: *Lectionary for Mass: Sundays, Solemnities, Feasts of the Lord and the Saints, Study Edition*. Chicago: Liturgy Training Publications.

Canada: *Lectionary for Mass: Sundays and Solemnities, Study Edition*. Ottawa: Canadian Conference of Catholic Bishops.

The advantage of these editions is that the text follows the sense-line formatting of the ritual editions used during Mass, making it easier for both comprehension and proclamation. Furthermore, when any of the texts are read aloud during dismissal prayer or extended catechesis, they should be read with the same art and skill as by the reader during Mass. These books may also be used year after year until the respective conference seeks a change in the biblical translation.

As an aid, dioceses may offer in the fall of each year an overview on the principal gospel of the coming liturgical year. If they do not, ask for it. Pastors or faith formation directors can host a quick overview for each season throughout the course of the year for all catechists, surely, but open to all adults as well.

Roman Missal

Study editions:

USA: Liturgical Press publishes a study edition (paperback) of the Missal that matches the page numbering of the hardbound (ritual) edition. The ritual editions by Liturgy Training Publications and the USCCB follow this same pagination. Other editions, regrettably, do not.

USA: World Library Publications has a small hand missal with ribbons and two-color ink.

Annual Publications with Lectionary and Missal Texts

Give Us This Day with monthly issues is published by Liturgical Press. It has the Lectionary and Missal texts arranged in the order used at Mass for each Sunday and weekday. Other pluses: daily reflection, a saint or holy person for each weekday, religious art, additional prayers, and a short guide to *lectio divina*.

Saint Joseph's Sunday Missal, Canadian edition, is an annual publication with prayers, readings, and responses in the order used for Mass.

Rite of Christian Initiation of Adults

See the Rites Belonging to the Period of the Catechumenate (RCIA 81–105; Canada, 81–104).

Helpful Resources

Christian Raab, OSB. "A Guide to Lectio Divina: God's Word Made Alive." St. Meinrad, IN: Abbey Press, 2009.

> Eight pages address things to keep in mind; things to keep at heart; and the who, what, where, when, and how of the method.

Luke Dysinger, OSB. "Guide to *Lectio Divina*" in each issue of *Give Us This Day*.

> One-page synopsis of the method.

Workbook for Lectors, Gospel Readers, and Proclaimers of the Word. Chicago: Liturgy Training Publications, annual.

> Separate editions for the USA (NABRE translation) and Canada (NRSV translation). Provides tips for good proclamation as well as some commentary on each of the readings. Sense-line formatting consistent with the ambo edition.

Liturgical Song Book

Because Roman Catholic liturgy is fundamentally a sung public prayer, ministers should also have access to the parish repertory and the music books used by the assembly. Because Roman Catholic liturgy is fundamentally a sung liturgy, ritual praying within catechumenal sessions should also include song, even if it is sung a cappella.

Structure and Design of the *Lectionary for Mass* for Sundays and Other Important Days

Volume 1 of the *Lectionary for Mass* in both the US and Canadian editions presents the texts for every Sunday as well as holydays of obligation, other solemnities, and feasts of the Lord that sometimes are celebrated on a Sunday in Ordinary Time. It is organized in a three-year pattern. Year A uses Matthew as the principal gospel, Year B uses Mark, and Year C uses Luke. Here is a couplet to determine the given liturgical year:

Liturgical Year C
is divisible by three.

Therefore, a remainder of one equals Year A and a remainder of two equals Year B. For example, 2019 was Year C because 2019 divided by three is a whole number. Also remember that Advent, the start of the new liturgical year, is always in late November or December of the preceding calendar year.

Seasons of Advent, Christmas, Lent, and Easter	Ordinary Time
Each season celebrates an aspect of the mystery of Christ. See chapter 3 of part I, "Sunday and the Liturgical Year," for greater details.	Thirty-three or thirty-four weeks that explore the holiness of the church by unfolding some dimension of the reign and kingdom of God.
■ **Advent** recalls the two comings of Christ. The Second Coming is the one for which we look and work. The first is promise of the second.	Some solemnities and feasts, because they are higher rank, replace a Sunday in Ordinary Time:
■ **Christmas Time** revels in the coming of Christ as a human, as one like us in all things but sin.	■ Presentation of the Lord, February 2
	■ Nativity of St. John the Baptist, June 24
■ **Lent** is preparation time for those to be baptized and renewal time for those already baptized. It is forty days for praying, fasting, and giving.	■ Sts. Peter and Paul, Apostles, June 29
	■ Transfiguration of the Lord, August 6

Seasons of Advent, Christmas, Lent, and Easter	Ordinary Time
■ **The Paschal Triduum** is the very heart of the church year. These three days annually recall our redemption in the paschal mystery of Jesus Christ the Lord.	■ Assumption of the Blessed Virgin Mary, August 15
	■ Exaltation of the Holy Cross, September 14
■ **Easter Time** is the fifty days to revel in that risen reality of life in Christ.	■ All Saints, November 1
	■ Commemoration of the Faithful Departed (All Souls), November 2
■ **Ordinary Time** celebrates the holiness of the church in many ways.	■ Dedication of the Lateran Basilica, November 9
	■ Parish solemnities of the patron of the church and of its dedication
■ **Gospel:** a reading from the principal gospel of the year or, in some instances, from John's gospel, chosen to be in harmony with the season.	■ **Gospel:** a semicontinuous reading of the principal gospel of the year, with some inserts from John's gospel.
■ **First Reading:** chosen to be in harmony with the gospel. It comes from the Old Testament, except in Easter Time when it is from the Acts of the Apostles.	■ **First Reading:** chosen to be in harmony with the gospel. It comes from the Old Testament.
■ **Responsorial Psalm:** chosen to be in harmony with the first reading.	■ **Responsorial Psalm:** chosen to be in harmony with the first reading.
■ **Second Reading:** chosen to be in harmony with all the readings. It is from a New Testament letter or from Revelation in Easter Time of Year C.	■ **Second Reading:** a semicontinuous reading of a New Testament letter. If it is in harmony with the gospel and the first reading, it is by chance and not by design.

"In harmony" is the language of the Introduction to the *Lectionary for Mass*. When readings are in harmony, to continue the musical analogy, they sing the same tune, they are in the same key, they tell the same story.

Responsorial psalm describes the manner in which the psalm is sung. The cantor sings the refrain, the assembly repeats it, the cantor sings a verse, the assembly repeats the refrain, and so on.

"Semicontinuous reading" starts at the beginning of the gospel or letter and continues each week, skipping parts that are read during Advent, Christmas, Lent, and Easter, as well as less important parts.

Step 2

Consulting with Some Liturgical Ministers

Story: Never Working Alone

In every one of my church jobs, from first to last, I never worked completely alone. What a blessing! Although I often had tasks that no one else could or should do, there were overlaps. In the parish, I could not finish the worship aid without consulting with the music director. I could not write the Sunday description for the bulletin without working with the priests on the homily focus and with the director for faith formation on the catechetical thrust for the age-specific groups. I could not participate in homily preparation without reviewing the Sunday texts and the liturgical year. This was best done when all of us stayed attuned to the people whom we served.

> ### John Hofinger, SJ, "Catechesis and Liturgy"
> How closely the catechetical and liturgical movements are allied, today more than ever . . . the two movements were on friendly terms from their very beginnings and proved mutually

helpful . . . It is in the liturgy above all that the Christian mysteries can in the course of the year be learned by "doing" them; they can become a living experience by taking part in them. (*Worship*, December 1954–January 1955, vol. 29, 2, pp. 89–95)

Collaborating Is Essential to Church Ministry

Collaboration is required to do church ministry effectively. It is more than mere cooperation. It is also more difficult. But the end product is richer. The General Instruction of the Roman Missal makes this clear about preparing to celebrate any Mass. No one person, from priest to musician to catechumenate director, acts alone. No one. We are reminded that the "pastoral effectiveness of a celebration will be greatly increased if the texts of the readings, the prayers, and the liturgical chants correspond as aptly as possible to the needs, the preparation, and the culture of the participants" (352). Then, this demand is made: attend to the spiritual good of the people of God rather than one's own desires or inclinations. What is said for Mass can be applied to all liturgy and to all related catechesis.

General Instruction of the Roman Missal

The pastoral effectiveness of a celebration will be greatly increased if the texts of the readings, the prayers, and the liturgical chants correspond as aptly as possible to the needs, the preparation, and the culture of the participants. This will be achieved by appropriate use of the many possibilities of choice described below.

Hence in arranging the celebration of Mass, the Priest should be attentive rather to the common spiritual good of the People of God than to his own inclinations. He should also remember that choices of this kind are to be made in harmony with those who exercise some part in the celebration, including the faithful, as regards the parts that more directly pertain to them.

Since, indeed, many possibilities are provided for choosing the different parts of the Mass, it is necessary for the Deacon, the readers, the psalmist, the cantor, the commentator, and the choir to know properly before the celebration the texts that concern each and that are to be used, and it is necessary that nothing be in any sense improvised. For harmonious ordering and carrying out of the rites will greatly help in disposing the faithful for participation in the Eucharist. (352)

In light of these charges, here are some specifics for those involved in the baptismal catechumenate during the second period.

First, catechumenal ministry cannot be seen, much less perceived, as a siloed, isolated aspect of church ministry. All catechetical and liturgical ministry is collaborative. Just as an auto shop will have specialists for tires, tune-ups, engine repair, and body work, they know how to work together and in proper order so that tasks do not have to be redone. The same is true in the church. I am aware that many baptismal catechumenate ministers are volunteers with essential duties off the parish campus at work and at home. Adequate preparation for dismissal and catechetical tasks may require two or three weeks to prepare. Thus, this collaboration cannot be last-day, last-minute work.

Second, the parish staff can help to facilitate this collaboration by seeing that sketches or pictures of the seasonal environment and art plan are accessible, if possible. Same for the music plan because the psalm refrain or opening song may be reprised in the dismissal or catechetical session or raised by catechumens in their reflection on the Sunday celebration.

Third, the parish staff can make accessible the parish calendar for the special or occasional things that will take place on Sunday. Special prayer texts, too. For example, what will occur with the blessing of the Advent wreath, the Jesse tree, the crèche in December? The blessing of candles and throats in February? The blessing of St. Joseph altars or Easter or Thanksgiving foods? The blessing of scouts, graduates, mothers and fathers, catechists on the third weekend of September, and liturgical ministers?

Fourth, preaching topics may be a little more difficult to access because that is generally a preparation done week by week. Be practical. True stories may help. In my experience, we had a parochial vicar that I called on Tuesday for a brief conversation. I began, "Here is the chosen topic based on our catechumens' discerned needs and the three or four highlights I have for the catechetical session." He could always give me the gist of his preaching. Sometimes I made some change; often I did not. But we were both aware of what the other was going to do. Our pastor, however, after two or three telephone calls, still was not sure of his preaching focus on Friday. I still called, just in case, but carried a 3x5 card to Mass to jot some key notes—so I would not forget—during his homily.

Here is an actual plan from a small two-hundred-household parish that was the only Catholic church in the county. Each Tuesday, the pastor, liturgist-RCIA director, the dismissal minister and catechumenal catechist, and part-time youth minister plus the volunteer child catechist and the children's Liturgy of the Word minister would gather in the rectory. It began with dinner (the pastor liked to cook, and "everybody needs to eat," he would say). The pastor then gave a short exposé on the readings with helpful connections to the season and the preceding and following Sundays. He then gave a brief outline of his homily. The musician gave a copy of the music plan. Catechists gave briefs on the catechetical plans for catechumens, children, and youth. The conversation that followed would note similarities, possible changes, but recognized that the homily must address everyone while catechesis for smaller groups might have more focused needs. This was two and a half to three hours well spent.

Practical Tips

The baptismal catechumenate director can be the conduit for passing along the art and environment plans, the liturgical music list, and any additions for a given week.

The dismissal minister and the catechist(s) can touch base on plans and outlines over coffee or a brief telephone call.

Do not be afraid to touch base with the preacher. Use the method that works best: telephone call, text message, or e-mail.

Helpful Resources

Fulfilled in Your Hearing: The Homily in the Sunday Assembly. USCCB, Subcommittee on Priestly Life and Ministry, 1982.

Although written for preachers and readers of the Word of God, the steps and methods will also aid catechists. Steps for the homiletic method, 78–105:

1. Reading, Listening, Praying

2. Study and Further Reflection

3. Letting Go

4. Drafting

5. Revising

6. Practicing

7. Preaching (and catechizing)

Preparation Group, 106–108, to include clergy, staff, and parishioners:

1. Read the passages (fifteen minutes)

2. Share the words (ten minutes)

3. Exegete (reflect on) the texts (ten minutes)

4. Share the good news (ten minutes)

5. Share the challenge these words offer us (ten minutes)

6. Explore the consequences (five minutes)

7. Give thanks and praise (five minutes)

Consulting with Past and Future Weeks

Story: Gardening in Zone 6

I am working at becoming a better gardener. It is a never-ending task that takes time and discernment. In the weeks of spring, I am always looking backward and forward. The beds are prepared as best they could be before the hard frost of winter. Dead annuals are removed. Compost is added where needed. Old bulbs in need of lifting are divided and reset while new bulbs for end-of-winter blooming are planted. Garlic, too, in another bed. Adjustments are made depending on the timing of early and hard frosts.

In the spring, the plan is for seed potatoes to go into the one-foot trench on Good Friday or the earlier feast of St. Patrick to honor the Irish. But because the former is a moveable day, I learn to attend to the weather and adjust the plan as needed. If I did not get the garlic in last fall, it is planted now.

In Plant Hardiness Zone 6, where I live, tomato seedlings are planted the first week of May. Beans and peppers follow. A few herbs a little later. But this always depends on the April showers, the moisture in the beds, the ambient and ground temperatures, and whether the planting is in a level or raised bed.

There is always a fall and a spring plan. But the plans depend on what happens before and what is predicted for the future.

Attending to the Parish Plans

Because the baptismal catechumenate team is regularly discerning the needs of the current catechumens (as well as the uncatechized Catholics for completing initiation with Confirmation and Eucharist and the baptized candidates for reception into full communion), the Sunday plan may be in draft form two or three months out at most, but surely not for the whole year. Those whom we serve now will not have the exact same concerns and needs as past catechumens and candidates.

The catechumenal catechist for a chosen week needs to know what was planned for the preceding few weeks and what happened, since an audible may be called (to use a football analogy) based on real-life needs.

The catechist also needs to know the focus for the coming week or two. This will prevent "dumping the whole load" of what we believe on a topic when it will be spread out over the coming weeks and in incremental fashion throughout the year.

For example, the Johannine interlude on the bread of life provides a five-week progression on Eucharist in August in Year B of St. Mark. Consider the parables that unfold the kingdom of heaven recounted by St. Matthew in the 15-17th Sundays in Ordinary Time of Year A. Consider also that forgiveness, for example, is addressed a handful of times in the year and not all at once.

In the vision and spirit of RCIA 75—that fourfold training and formation plan for the period of the catechumenate—what else is going on in parish life, what else are parishioners involved in off the parish campus that should include the participation of catechumens and candidates with the rest of the faithful? What can be, should be taking place in the homes? What mercy and justice work is being done and still needs to be done?

This step will not take long. It is important, however, because no single Sunday, no liturgical week, no catechumenal week stands completely alone.

Drafting a Suitable Focus

Story: Planning for College

The plan for our son's college years was a family endeavor with short and long-term details and goals. For the long-term, my wife and I looked at setting aside funds (meager though they were, we discovered) long before our son was even aware college was a desire or possibility. We had to make changes to this goal as he got older. His own high school years helped to shape his intentions post-graduation. His choice of one of the two junior colleges in town helped him further refine his goals and shift his focus. This helped to shape short-term goals of choice of degree, college, housing, and part-time job. Changes were made at each stage along the way.

Focusing and Planning for a Given Week

Some of the praying and consulting in the previous steps may be done weeks in advance. Some will necessarily be done closer to the chosen Sunday. Some catechists, those volunteers with full-time jobs off the parish campus and those relatively new to this ministry, will need two, three, or four weeks to work on the session.

But before looking at a resource with a complete session plan for a given week, based on the Sunday texts, surely, written by someone from a far-away place, it is essential to know the local catechumens' needs first. Step 7 will discuss why a method for designing sessions is better than relying on resources with complete sessions prepared elsewhere and often long ago.

Example of the Nineteenth Week in Ordinary Time, Year A

An example may help. The *long-term plan* set by the Lectionary itself for any week in Ordinary Time is an unfolding of some aspect of living within the reign and kingdom of God now and working to bring it to fruition with God's good help. If the assignment is the Nineteenth Sunday in Ordinary Time, Year A, we would also want to be aware of at least the two weeks that surround it.

Liturgical Year A	Theme Possibilities
Eighteenth Sunday in Ordinary Time (no. 112A)	Withdrawing for prayer
Isaiah 55:1-3: *Hasten and eat.*	God's abundance and generosity
Psalm 145:8-9, 15-16, 17-18 (cf. 16): The hand of the Lord feeds us; he answers all our needs.	The promise of covenant, God's loving-kindness
	God satisfies our real needs
Romans 8:35, 37-39: *No creature will be able to separate us from the love of God in Jesus Christ.*	Feeding the many
	Foreshadowing Eucharist
Matthew 14:13-21: *They all ate and were satisfied.*	SECOND READING: Christ loves us
	No person or thing can separate us from Christ
Nineteenth Sunday in Ordinary Time (no. 115A)	
	God's revelation
1 Kings 19:9a, 11-13a: *Go outside and stand on the mountain before the Lord.*	Withdrawing for prayer
	God speaks in the quiet
Psalm 85:9, 10, 11-12, 13-14 (8): Lord, let us see your kindness, and grant us your salvation.	God quiets the storm
	Do not be afraid, Christ is with us

Romans 9:1-5: *I could wish that I were accursed for the sake of my own people.*

Matthew 14:22-33: *Command me to come to you on the water.*

SECOND READING:
Concerns for the People of God

Twentieth Sunday in Ordinary Time (no. 118A)

Isaiah 56:1, 6-7: *I will bring foreigners to my holy mountain.*

Psalm 67:2-3, 5, 6, 8 (4): O God, let all the nations praise you!

Romans 11:13-15, 29-32: *The gifts and the call of God for Israel are irrevocable.*

Matthew 15:21-28: *O woman, great is your faith!*

Great faith

Relentlessly seeking Christ's help

Do what is right and just

No one is a foreigner to God's covenant, love, and mercy

SECOND READING:
God's loving-kindness, mercy, covenant

The *short-term plan* set by the parish, attending to the discerned needs of the current catechumens and candidates, will distill the possibilities. Here are two examples. Notice that neither plan addresses all the possibilities just as good homilies cannot and do not.

Parish Plan A

Eighteenth Sunday in Ordinary Time (no. 112A)

The Eucharist is our greatest prayer: about your longing and preparing for it.

Nineteenth Sunday in Ordinary Time (no. 115A)

Listening for God's voice and seeing God/Christ active in our lives.

Twentieth Sunday in Ordinary Time (no. 118A)

Seeking Christ's help early and often.

Parish Plan B

Eighteenth Sunday in Ordinary Time (no. 112A)

Nothing can separate us from Christ.

Nineteenth Sunday in Ordinary Time (no. 115A)

Do not fear anything, for Christ is with us.

Twentieth Sunday in Ordinary Time (no. 118A)

No one is foreign to relentless faith in Christ.

Drafting Questions

What are the current needs of the catechumens? Is there anything that is new and pressing? What support, if any, is there in the Sunday texts?

If the team has already chosen a suitable focus, how does my own prayer help to support it? Is it still suitable for the catechumens?

If it is left to me to choose the suitable focus, how does my praying with the texts and consulting the preaching and music plans of others help me to draft this short-term focus?

Although this will be addressed more intently in step 7, how can we pray in suitable ways using the Rites Belonging to the Period of the Catechumenate (RCIA 81–105; Canada, 81–104)?

The Draft

Drafting a suitable focus for the Nineteenth Sunday in Ordinary Time, Year A, may look like this:

Parish Plan A

Listening for God's voice and seeing God/Christ active in our lives.

Subpoints:

- Even when running away from life's turmoil, I cannot run from God.
- God is always speaking, always present.
- Time away for silent prayer; retreat day.
- Reprise from Sunday Mass "O God, You Search Me" by Bernadette Farrell *or* "Precious Lord, Take My Hand" by Thomas Dorsey *or* "How Can I Keep from Singing?" by Robert Lowry.
- Consider using either Minor Exorcism A or Blessing D or I from the Rites Belonging to the Period of the Catechumenate.

Parish Plan B

Do not fear anything, for Christ is with us.

Subpoints:

- Storms, tumult, and tragedy happen but are not more powerful than Christ.
- Christ always invites us to come to him; he is with us all the time.
- Reprise from Sunday Mass "You Are Mine" by David Haas *or* "How Firm a Foundation" by John Rippon *or* "Eternal Father, Strong to Save" by William Whiting.
- Consider using either Minor Exorcism A or G or Blessing E. Anointing of the Catechumens may be celebrated by a priest or deacon.

Step 5

Uncovering the Meaning of the Texts

Story: Getting It Wrong and Making It Right

When I worked at Sacred Heart of Jesus in New Orleans, Louisiana, the staff and parish council officers regularly met with eight other parishes to share and work on team ministry concerns. The group even contracted a church management group for eight sessions over two years to sharpen our skills.

Fr. George told this story about getting things right. The team was working on an organizational development project for St. John the Baptist parish some years back. It was only in the weeks prior to the training date, in conversation with the local leaders, that the team realized that "parish" in this instance was not a religious one, but a "civil" one—civil parish in Louisiana is akin to county in the rest of the country. To get this wrong corrected, they had to rethink the presentations, agenda, and handouts.

United States Conference of Catholic Bishops,
United States Catholic Catechism for Adults,
Appendix A, Glossary

EXEGESIS: The process used by Scripture scholars to determine the literal and spiritual meanings of the biblical texts.
See chapter 3, "Proclaim the Gospel to Every Creature."

Grasping the True Meaning of the Texts

It is always the desire that the planning in steps 1 through 4 is
right on the money. It is possible, however, that the fundamental
focus of the chosen week is slightly wrong or completely wrong.
Here is where *exegesis* helps. This is the scholarly word that describes the process to uncover the meaning of the text. Here is an
instance why this is important.

We read and hear Mark 10:2-16 on the Twenty-Seventh Sunday
in Ordinary Time, Year B (LM 140B). It begins with the question
about the legality of divorce as a test of Jesus and a response by
him. The Lectionary gives this citation as the focus of the reading:
"Therefore what God has joined together, let no human being
separate." The final verses, however, focus on children. The
crowds bring the children to Jesus, the disciples rebuke this, Jesus
says, "Let the children come to me . . ."

I have heard homilies based on this latter part of the gospel
about the need to love and support children because Jesus does
it and wants us to do the same. While this is consistent with Christian values, John Pilch tells us something different about first-
century life and experience:

> Children were walking newspapers of that time. They were
> trained by their families and permitted by other families to roam
> freely in and out of homes to spy on what other families were
> doing. Attempts to keep children away from Jesus would stir
> suspicions that he was up to no good and intent on harming
> others. Jesus insists he has nothing to hide. Let the children

snoop. (*The Cultural World of Jesus: Sunday by Sunday, Cycle B*, Collegeville, MN: Liturgical Press, 1996, pp. 146–147)

The point here is that Jesus is transparent and has nothing to hide; that what he says and does in private, he does and says in public. This would foster a very different homily and catechetical session.

Testing the Draft Focus

The appendix contains an extended annotated bibliography of many resources for this and remaining steps. It begins on page 141. All the items listed are good. However, all of them need not be consulted each planning week nor can they be. But it shows the vast information available to help uncover the true meaning of biblical texts. See what is available in the parish library or used by parish staff. Seek out an author and writing style that suits your needs.

Find the way to make these works accessible. Two examples may help.

One: The catechumenate team in my parish has a cupboard for its library in the school meeting room used for dismissal prayer and extended catechesis. It is accessible on Sunday and on any day the school is open for team members to get and return books.

Two: There is a cluster of two very small rural parishes in the diocese, each with a business district of two blocks. The parishes have limited office space, and buildings are open on a limited basis during the week. They have a joint catechumenal team of four. The working library is in a plastic crate kept in a member's car trunk. Every Sunday it is available to team members to return what was used and borrow what is needed.

Three Helpful Resources among Many

Let us look at three books among the list of "Some works to CONSULT FIRST" from the bibliography in the appendix for a review of the Nineteenth Sunday in Ordinary Time, Year A, sample draft.

John J. Pilch, *The Cultural World of Jesus: Sunday by Sunday, Year A*

Pilch has a series of books addressing all the Sunday readings that helps today's reader to look at the texts with first-century eyes. Start with the books on the gospels. For the Nineteenth Sunday in Ordinary Time, Year A, in three pages, Pilch addresses fishing, spirits and storms, and prayer. In the second topic, he asserts that wind spirits can wreak havoc on human life. It is God through Christ who is more powerful than evil and mischievous spirits. The draft focus examples of both parish plans in step 4 are consistent with his research.

Dianne Bergant with Richard Fragomeni, *Preaching the New Lectionary, Year A*

Bergant situates the Nineteenth Sunday within the cluster encompassing the Eighteenth through Twenty-Fourth Sundays. She provides a helpful chart and a three-page summary of this set of readings. In six pages, Bergant provides commentary on all the biblical texts for this Sunday. She ends with these themes for the day: the whispering sound, subdue chaos, concern for others. These first and second themes are consistent with the draft focus for both parish plans in step 4.

Roland Faley, *Footprints on the Mountain: Preaching and Teaching the Sunday Readings*

This is a single volume for all three years. In five pages, Faley begins with a theme of "a peaceful presence" in the opening paragraph. He then provides commentary on each biblical text. He ends with this list of Homiletic and Catechetical Helps for the Nineteenth Sunday in Ordinary Time, Year A.

1. Christ's presence with the church.
2. The importance of a trusting faith.
3. The value of silence in our lives.
4. The significance of retreats and days of recollection.
5. Peter: the importance of stepping out in faith.
6. Peter: doubt in the face of difficulty.
7. The Jews in God's saving plan.
8. Prayer for and with our Jewish neighbors.
9. Positive attitudes regarding other faiths.
10. Our shared heritage with the Jews.

Faley's numbers 1 to 3 and 5 to 6 support the draft focus of parish plan A in step 4. Number 4 may make some connection to a parish recollection day set for the future or prompt a desire to plan one. Numbers 2, 5, and 6 support the draft focus of parish plan B.

This step does not have to be an exhausting one. It does help us to be faithful—faithful to the real meaning of the biblical texts as well as faithful to the needs of the catechumens with whom we journey in faith.

Step 6

Redrafting the Focus

Questions and Ongoing Discernment

After uncovering the meaning of the Lectionary texts through some biblical scholarship, there is the need to ask at least two questions.

1. What adjustments are needed on the chosen focus because of this study and exegesis?

2. What best meets the needs of the church and the catechumenal community?

The answers may be that no adjustments are required and that needs are being met, or the answers may be that we missed the mark a lot or a little. The questions need asking. Revisions follow as needed.

If we look at the examples for the Nineteenth Sunday in Ordinary Time, Year A, in the previous step 4 with the helpful review in step 5, we see some alternative possibilities for preaching and for catechesis. Bergant offers concern for others. Faley offers interfaith and ecumenical concerns. Even though, in these examples, the chosen focus is consistent with the review of biblical commentary, something may be happening in the catechumens' lives and conversations that may warrant a shift in the focus.

Perhaps a catechumen is still quite self-centered, still thinks that God and me alone are enough to be religious. In that case, there may be the need to address the concern for others, the need for discipleship that Bergant exposes out of the second reading.

Perhaps a catechumen has difficulty believing that God loves all people of faith, even those who are not Christian, that God loves all believers, and that God could love all people, period. The suggestions that Faley has toward the end of his list may need addressing instead of the original draft focus.

What determines either keeping the draft focus or shifting it is honest ongoing discernment of the current catechumens. It is never determined by what I like, by what I want, by what the catechumenate director alone thinks, or by what was prepared last time this Sunday occurred, even if I did the preparation.

Just as with good preaching, good catechesis addresses the catechumenal needs in light of one or more possibilities that the church presents.

Helpful Resource

The following work is noted in the extensive list in chapter 5. A regular review of "Discernment in the Catechumenal Period," pp. 47–58, is helpful. It is only a dozen pages.

Donna Steffen, SC. *Discernment in Christian Initiation*. Chicago: Liturgy Training Publications, 2018.

> Revises the previous editions of her book *Discerning Disciples: Listening for God's Voice in Christian Initiation*. Describes the decision-making process, serves to improve the listening skills, and helps to ask the right questions at the right time. The appendix contains specific suggestions for interviews during the four stages of the catechumenate and offers a format for a discernment day before the Rite of Election.

Step 7

Designing the Week

Story: Telling the Whole Truth

In my diocesan work, I regularly encountered parish catechumenate teams not addressing all of the fourfold apprenticeship needs of catechumens: "the pastoral formation and guidance, aimed at training them in the Christian life" (RCIA 75). In workshops as well as in parish conversations, I presented some version of the following.

Open your ritual book to RCIA 75. The formation and training in this period, whose goal is conversion and conformation to Christ, is achieved by four necessities. If truth be told, most places spend time on the first, catechesis, whether it is suitable or not, bad or good. How much time and effort are being devoted to the other three?

We learn the Christian way of life by hanging around with many more Christians than those on staff and team. Catechumens need guided exposure to everything in which parishioners are involved. Who would marry someone, for example, without spending time with the in-laws (and outlaws)?

Although all participate in the first part of Sunday Mass, these Introductory Rites and Liturgy of the Word are not enough. Every time catechumens gather, there needs to be prayer. Not just any prayer and not just a single Our Father, for example. What is needed is liturgical prayer with reading, song, prayer, and silence. This period provides a model structure and examples in the ritual book.

Catechumens learn the apostolic life by doing and saying the things Christians say and do while alongside them off the parish campus.

If these four elements are equally important, and they are, then over the span of any four to six weeks, we should be able to allot 25 percent of our time and effort for each one. It may be heavy on catechesis one week and heavy on apostolic life for another, but over each short term, we spend roughly equal time on each of the four.

How is your parish doing? It usually gets very quiet in the room. The truth telling often results in this: heavy on one, light on the rest.

Then I ask: What was the participation in all eight weeks of mystagogy last Easter Time? If neophytes stop showing up after a couple weeks, it is my experience and belief that the whole period of the catechumenate was too short (not a whole liturgical year or more to unwrap the entire mystery of Christ) and probably not focused on all four elements for that training and formation.

Then we talk about short-term strategies by asking more questions. How can we help catechumens to see aspects of this formation already present in their lives by suitable open-ended questions, reflection, and conversation? How can we tie this to the Sunday by reprising some text or song? How can we pray in suitable ways? See Rites Belonging to the Period of the Catechumenate (RCIA 81–105; Canada, 81–104) with:

- Celebrations of the Word of God

- Minor Exorcisms

- Blessings of the Catechumens

- Anointing of the Catechumens (optional in Canada)

- Presentations (optional in this period)

Using All the Elements for the Design

In the helpful resources section in part I, chapter 4, on pages 61–62, six items are given for suitable catechetical methods. Let us look at the two sample parish plans using Groome's shared Christian praxis. The value of this method, and the others cited with it, is a respect for the way adults learn. It is consistent with what the *National Directory for Catechesis* posits in Section 29. We learn faith in many ways. Delivery of information is not the only way, nor is it usually first in presentation. Faith is learned, faith is informed by human experience. It is formed by exercising discipleship. It is formed within the community of believers and the Christian family.

Although Groome's language seems written in the style of a doctoral dissertation, it is still worth reading and using this valuable method. Some simpler language, however, may help us to get to the heart of this method.

Praxis: a practice, a way of doing something, not a theory.

See Thomas Groome, *Sharing Faith: A Comprehensive Approach to Religious Education and Pastoral Ministry—The Way of Shared Praxis*. Part II explains the steps in detail.

See Gilbert Ostdiek, *Catechesis for Liturgy: A Program for Parish Involvement*. Chapter 1, in presenting an outline of his own method, Ostdiek offers a nice summary of Groome's method.

Shared Christian Praxis Method

Groome Language	"Easy" Language
◆ Focusing activity in shared praxis	◆ Focusing on a common topic or story
1. Naming/Expressing "Present Action"	1. **What are you doing?** ■ Your story
2. Critical Reflection on Present Action	2. **Why do you do that?** ■ Your underlying assumptions

3. Making Accessible Christian Story and Vision	**3. What is the Christian tradition?** ■ The Christian story and vision ■ The "bigger" picture
4. Dialectical Hermeneutic to Appropriate Christian Story/Vision to Participants' Stories and Visions	**4. What might we learn from dialogue?** ■ Your story and big story in conversation
5. Decision/Response for Lived Christian Faith	**5. What are you going to do now?** ■ Affirmation—Insight ■ Challenge—Conversion

Designing the Week

Let us work on the two draft parish plans from chapter 4 for the Nineteenth Sunday in Ordinary Time, Year A, a Sunday that occurs in mid-August. In real parish life, ministers will make only one plan. Two are presented here to demonstrate possibilities because there is always more than one focus possible. There is always so much information that we must choose some and omit others.

Parish Plan A

Listening for God's voice and seeing God/Christ active in our lives.

Subpoints:

♦ Even when running away from life's turmoil, I cannot run from God.

♦ God is always speaking, always present.

♦ Time away for silent prayer; retreat day.

♦ Reprise from Sunday Mass "O God, You Search Me" by Bernadette Farrell *or* "Precious Lord, Take My Hand" by Thomas Dorsey *or* "How Can I Keep from Singing?" by Robert Lowry.

♦ Consider using either Minor Exorcism A or Blessing D or I from the Rites Belonging to the Period of the Catechumenate.

Parish Plan B

Do not fear anything, for Christ is with us.

Subpoints:

♦ Storms, tumult, and tragedy happen but are not more powerful than Christ.

♦ Christ always invites us to come to him; he is with us all the time.

♦ Reprise from Sunday Mass "You Are Mine" by David Haas *or* "How Firm a Foundation" by John Rippon *or* "Eternal Father, Strong to Save" by William Whiting.

♦ Consider using either Minor Exorcism A or G or Blessing I. Anointing of the Catechumens may be celebrated by a priest or deacon.

In designing the week, attend to all the elements of RCIA 75, because suitable catechesis, community living, prayer and liturgy, and apostolic living are essential for catechumenal formation and training. Start to work on the design with Groome step 3.

Groome Step 3

This is the input step of accessing the Christian story. Here we access doctrine and tradition in partial ways accommodated to the Lectionary readings, the season of the year, and the catechumens' own journey of faith. It is the step that will share "This is what Catholics know and believe."

Parish Plan A	**Parish Plan B**
Listening for God's voice and seeing God/Christ active in our lives.	*Do not fear anything, for Christ is with us.*

In the preceding verses of today's reading, Elijah mocks and shames the queen's prophets, enrages Jezebel, and runs away to save his very life. He is fed and nourished by God on this long run to Horeb (Sinai), God's holy mountain. In today's reading, in the shelter of this place apart, God passes by in an unexpected way requiring Elijah's attention. He stands at the entrance of the cave, in the reveal of the doorway, for God's revelation.

Jesus, too, goes off alone to be with God, to pray.

Elijah's experience urges us to get away, to take shelter, to be silent at times so that we can hear God speak and see God active in our lives.

Nothing is so insignificant that it does not show the presence of God in my life, in our lives, and the world.

Read the first reading.

Follow with silence.

In today's gospel, Jesus walks on water to the foundering disciples' boat. He says, "Take courage, it is I; do not be afraid." Peter walks on water but sinks and cries, "Lord, save me!" Jesus chides such little faith, grabs hold of Peter, and stills the storm.

What does it mean that Jesus Christ saves us—salvation, redemption, paschal mystery?

We are saved once and for all—and every day—by him and his saving action.

Jesus's post-resurrection, Easter message: do not fear, peace be with you, the Advocate/Spirit and I are with you always.

Therefore, we have nothing really to fear, for this life is journey to heavenly life.

Here are examples of martyrs (those who give up their lives for what and in whom they believe) long ago and in our current day. From Scripture: Maccabees brothers and mother (2 Macc 7); Stephen (Acts 7–8). From the current calendar: St. Teresa Benedicta of the Cross (August 9), and St. Maximillian Kolbe (August 14).

Have all stand and hear the gospel read aloud.

Follow with some silence.

Then ask, what strikes you now?

After the conversation, close with the refrain from "You Are Mine."

A faithful catechist will generally prepare more things than can be said on the topic in the allotted time but is always prepared not to say them all—not to dump the whole load, as it were. What is said and not said will be shaped by Groome's focusing topic and steps 1 and 2. We design them next in light of the input piece of step 3.

Groome Focusing Topic or Story

Here we tap into the real human experience of the participants that relates to the doctrine of step 3 in a non-doctrinal way. Note that this topic and steps 1 and 2 are participant focused. Since they call on personal experience, there are no wrong answers.

Parish Plan A	Parish Plan B
Listening for God's voice and seeing God/Christ active in our lives.	*Do not fear anything, for Christ is with us.*
Listening can be hard.	Being afraid and being courageous. For example, the Cowardly Lion in *The Wizard of Oz*; Jean Valjean in *Les Misérables*; civil rights preachers, marchers, and workers.

A shift in Parish Plan A is taken by our mythical parish. Instead of doing suitable catechesis, this week will focus on:

1. Sunday Mass with dismissal as usual.

2. Dismissal prayer as usual.

3. Not the extended catechesis that would follow either right after Mass or a later weeknight.

4. Participating, instead, in the celebration of the Anniversary of the Dedication of the Parish Church (a local solemnity) on Friday.

5. The parish calendar, provided weeks ago, notes this schedule:

   9:00 a.m.: Anniversary of Dedication Mass ending with exposition of the Eucharist for the morning and afternoon

   12:00 noon: Midday Prayer

   3:00 p.m.: Celebration of the Word of God

   5:30 p.m.: Evening Prayer including thirty minutes of silence ending with benediction and reposition of the Eucharist

   6:30 p.m.: Parish dinner

Catechumens already knew and saved this day long ago as all parishioners did. Two to three weeks prior to the Nineteenth Sunday, after short-term planning by the catechumenate team, this adjustment was made.

• Sunday gathering is over at the end of Dismissal Prayer and Mass.

• Catechumens meet up with their sponsors, with families, for the 5:30 p.m. Evening Prayer on Friday. They bring their journals and Bibles (for use during the long silence as needed).

• The team collaborated with the pastor to reprise the 1 Kings text from the Nineteenth Sunday as the reading.

- All stay for dinner.

- On the following Sunday, after dismissal prayer, mystagogical catechesis on the Liturgy of the Hours with exposition, benediction, and reposition replaces the usual extended catechesis.

Groome Step 1: What Is Your Story?

It helps if the catechist does her own reflection on this step in the planning. This will assist in setting up some prompts to get catechumens "on topic." Give a handful of ideas, including even your own, but without telling the whole story.

The sharing from small group to large is always by design. The smaller the group, the more comfort and safety there is to share. You want everyone to share in the smaller group so do not rush but also do not let this drag on. It is not necessary that everyone share in the large group.

Parish Plan B

Do not fear anything,
for Christ is with us.

Think of a time you were afraid. When your life was in peril.

For example, bullied at school or work; took a public and perhaps unpopular stand on an issue of ethics or justice; leaving a gang; heading into major surgery.

It could be something big or little in your life.

Take some alone time to fill in the details. Journal if helpful.

Then share what you wish:
- Catechumen-sponsor pairs,
- Small group of five or six,
- Whole group.

Groome Step 2: Reflection and Assumptions

The first questions and, thus, the beginning of conversation in step 2 help all participants to get underneath their own story. This is truth-telling. The answer to "Why?" may be "I have no idea." Or it may be very specific.

Be careful about trying to be too helpful, about filling in the blanks in others' stories. Silence is not a bad thing. It can mean I do not know, I do not want to share out loud, or it is so profound that I do not yet have words.

Parish Plan B

Do not fear anything, for Christ is with us.

Why did you do what you did?

Describe how you felt, your emotions. At the beginning; after it was over.

What does this tell you about fear? About protection? About being safe?

It may be helpful during this planning step to look at the appendix bibliography 7.3 on pages 148–149, especially if there is need for help in shaping reflective questions. If the topic and questions of a book are not related to your topic, put it quickly down and pick up another. Look for questions that do not ask for a simple yes or no, that are personal (I or me, not you or they), that focus on heart and hands activity rather than academic information. Change the words and pronouns as needed so they are in an open-ended form.

Insert next the previous work on Groome step 3 that began this designing. This does not have to be long and drawn out. Ten and fifteen minutes should be enough. Yes, that short! Remember, this is initiatory catechesis. This topic will come up one or two or ten more times in slightly differing contexts, perhaps, over the course of the liturgical year. Christ is gradually unfolded. Allow additional time for clarity, more questions, and any needed conversation.

If stuck on any of this designing, especially if you are new to this ministry, look to the appendix bibliography 7.4 on pages 149–150. These books will give you complete session outlines. Use them in the same way you used the books in the previous section. If one is not related to your chosen focus, put it down and go to another. It is not required that you use everything; use the portion that helps, use what supports and furthers the development of your chosen parish plan.

Why not just start here? All the work is done, some will say. Here are the reasons for not starting with these books. All of them were written a while ago by good, thoughtful, and competent people skilled in liturgy and catechesis who live far away. Although the writers all know and love catechumens, they do not know and love those who currently are in your care. Use what is helpful and insightful for your needs and skip what is not. As you become more and more comfortable with shared Christian praxis, or other suitable catechetical methods, you may find yourself relying less and less on session plans written by others.

If you and your team are new to this catechumenal catechesis and are nervous and unsure, then pick one volume that seems best suited to your people. Give yourself a three-year plan to wean away from regular use. If in the second year you are unhappy with the series, pick another one.

If you are a new catechist, and the team is experienced, work as pairs for a while until there is ease with the method.

Groome Step 4:
Conversation between My Story and the Big Story

This step 4, just like steps 1 and 2, centers on the participants. The questions need to be personal and open ended. In paying attention to all the preceding conversations, new and focused questions may be asked while always being careful not to embarrass or push too hard.

Talk and listen. Decide whether small-to-large group or large group alone is best.

Parish Plan B

*Do not fear anything,
for Christ is with us.*

How does the church story bump up against your own story of fear or peril?

How did God have a part, have a hand in your story, your experience?

Were you aware of God's presence during it? Only in reflecting on it afterward? Not at all?

What do you think now?

Groome Step 5: Now What?

This is also a participant-centered step. Ending the session on the agreed-upon time is essential. If enough time remains, the small or large group can continue with the following. If time is short, they can be posed with a bit of silence to start some personal reflection that can be completed at home.

Parish Plan B

*Do not fear anything,
for Christ is with us.*

What do I need to do or say or stop doing or saying to be more faithful?

What boat am I invited to step out of?

What are the dangerous waters on which I will walk?

What is Jesus asking of me? Of us? How is he saving me today?

What of my experience and belief has been affirmed by our work today?

What challenges me to rethink what I believe? What I do or not do?

End in prayer. Pick from Minor Exorcism A or G or Blessing I that best fits the conversation. Be open to doing something different based on what precedes.

A handout to take home may be welcomed. Type it up in holy card fashion, so it can be carried in purse or pocket.

Two that fit today's work: "How great the sign of God's love for us" from RCIA Appendix II, Hymns in the Style of the New Testament, 2. Using the sense-line format is required. By printing this copyright information at the bottom and by doing this as one-time-use (keeping only a file copy and recycling the rest), you do not need any additional permission—and you will not go to copyright jail:

Reprinted from the *Rite of Christian Initiation of Adults* © 1985, International Committee on English in the Liturgy Corporation. All rights reserved.

Or give the Prayer of St. Francis, "Make Me an Instrument of Your Peace."

End with brief announcements. What will happen this coming week. See you next Sunday.

A final point. Prayer can take place during any of the steps, especially steps 3, 4, and 5. It can also occur more than once.

Step 8

Sharing the Design

This last step is relatively easy. It is also collaborative.

1. With Whom Is This Design Shared?

When I am catechist, I generally have a handwritten outline (as neat as I am able) of one or two pages as my guide. I can photocopy or scan the pages to share with the catechists for the following week or two (so they know the plan that precedes them), with the team member in charge of discernment (to track which topics for which catechumens), and with the director (for the file). If I am really brave, I hand over my original text for the file because it will never be given in this exact way three years from now.

2. What Handouts Need to Be Prepared?
Are Copyright Permissions Needed?

If something is prepared to hand out, be sure it is legally reproduced or purchased. Include author and sourcing. Include it with the outline.

Appendix

Steps for Preparing a Week in the Period of the Catechumenate

(Including an Annotated Bibliography)

The Steps

1. PRAYING with the liturgical texts
2. CONSULTING with some of the liturgical ministries
3. CONSULTING with past and present and future weeks
4. DRAFTING a suitable focus
5. EXEGETING/UNCOVERING THE MEANING of the texts
6. REDRAFTING the focus
7. DESIGNING the week
8. SHARING the design

The Steps Explained

1. PRAYING with the liturgical texts

1. What are the Bible readings from the *Lectionary for Mass*?

2. What are the prayers and rites from *The Roman Missal*?

3. What is the solemnity or feast and the season (time) of the year?

4. What else will be celebrated: a blessing from the *Book of Blessings*, a prayer, or a sacrament? What other parish events will take place?

2. CONSULTING *with some of the liturgical ministries*

1. What MUSIC has been chosen, especially entrance song, introductory rites, responsorial psalm, and dismissal of catechumens?

2. What is the HOMILY focus, direction, or topic?

3. What ENVIRONMENT and ART is prepared for the day or the season?

3. CONSULTING *with past and present and future weeks*

1. What was the planned focus and what actually happened in each of the past few weeks?

2. What is the chosen focus for each of the coming few weeks?

3. How can this week complement the past and future weeks?

4. How does the ongoing discernment with catechumens and candidates by the catechumenate team and sponsors affect this preparation?

5. How do the past, present, and future weeks attend to all of RCIA 75?

4. DRAFTING *a suitable focus*

1. If the focus list is set for a long term, is the chosen focus still suitable?

2. If the focus list is set for a short term, what best meets the needs of the church and the catechumenal community?

5. EXEGETING/UNCOVERING THE MEANING of the texts

1. What help can textual scholarship provide for uncovering the meaning? Who can provide it?

2. Some works to CONSULT FIRST—pick one or two:

John J. Pilch. *The Cultural World of Jesus: Sunday by Sunday*. Three volumes. Collegeville, MN: Liturgical Press, Year A, 1995; Year B, 1996; Year C, 1997.

> Presents cultural reflections on the gospels; highlights aspects of the first century, Eastern Mediterranean world in which Jesus lived; helps readers to make applications of Scripture to modern life.

John J. Pilch. *The Triduum and Easter Sunday: Breaking Open the Scriptures*. Collegeville, MN: Liturgical Press, 2000.

> Supplement to the earlier work; treats all of the Scripture readings of the three days.

John J. Pilch. *The Cultural World of the Prophets: The First Reading and the Responsorial Psalm, Sunday by Sunday*. Three volumes. Collegeville, MN: Liturgical Press, Year A, 2004; Year B, 2003; Year C, 2003. *The Cultural World of the Apostles: The Second Reading, Sunday by Sunday*. Three volumes. Collegeville, MN: Liturgical Press, Year A, 2001; Year B, 2002; Year C, 2003.

> Cultural reflection as above; helps to identify plausible links with the gospel; helps to explore pastoral applications to modern life.

Dianne Bergant with Richard Fragomeni. *Preaching the New Lectionary*. Three volumes. Collegeville, MN: Liturgical Press, Year A, 2001; Year B, 1999; Year C, 2000.

> A literary-liturgical reading of the texts; situates the interpretation of each day within the theology of the season drawn from the themes of the readings.

Roland Faley. *Footprints on the Mountain: Preaching and Teaching the Sunday Readings*. Mahwah, NJ: Paulist Press, 1994.

> Commentary on all four readings for Sundays, for selected solemnities and feasts, as well as for weddings and funerals; reflection on implications for Christian life; and list of homiletic and catechetical topics.

Reginald H. Fuller and Daniel Westberg. *Preaching the Lectionary: The Word of God for the Church Today*. 3rd ed. Collegeville, MN: Liturgical Press, 2006.

Comments on all four readings for Sundays, for selected solemnities and feasts, as well as the readings for weddings and funerals. Suggestions on homily and catechetical possibilities.

Patricia Datchuck Sánchez. *The Word We Celebrate: Commentary on the Sunday Lectionary, Years A, B, and C.* Kansas City: Sheed & Ward, 1989.

Provides exegesis, background, and insights on the Scripture texts.

3. Some works to CONSULT SECOND:

Gerard S. Sloyan. *A Commentary on the New Lectionary.* New York: Paulist Press, 1975.

Combines homiletic and exegetical concerns; interprets the biblical texts on historical principles from the standpoint of Christian faith.

Adrian Nocent. *The Liturgical Year.* Four volumes. Collegeville, MN: Liturgical Press, 1977.

Treats both biblical and ritual texts in a three-part pattern: biblical and liturgical reflections, structure and themes, suggestions from the past. 1: Advent, Christmas, and Epiphany. 2: Lent and Holy Week. 3: The Easter Season. 4: Sundays in Ordinary Time.

Adrian Nocent. *The Liturgical Year.* Introduced, emended, and annotated by Paul Turner. Three volumes. Collegeville, MN: Liturgical Press, 2013–2014.

A modified version of the work noted above. Advent, Christmas, and Epiphany, 2013. Lent, the Sacred Paschal Triduum, and Easter Time, 2014. Sundays Two to Thirty-Four in Ordinary Time, 2013.

Days of the Lord: The Liturgical Year. Seven volumes. Collegeville, MN: Liturgical Press, 1991–1994.

Treats biblical and ritual texts for Sundays and weekdays, as well as the Liturgy of the Hours. Advent, Christmas, and Epiphany. Lent. Easter Triduum and Easter Season. Ordinary Time, Year A. Ordinary Time, Year B. Ordinary Time, Year C. Solemnities and Feasts.

Scripture Backgrounds for the Sunday Lectionary: A Resource for Homilists. Chicago: Liturgy Training Publications, Year A, 2016; Year B, 2017; Year C, 2018.

Resource for homilist and catechists with a common background to assist the meditation and presentation; with related quotes of church teaching and tradition.

4. Some works to CONSULT THIRD as time and interest allows:

Homily-Liturgy-Catechetical Resources. Much is available providing segments on some or all the following: exegesis, preaching, music, prayers, environment, and so on. Check with your pastor or parish life coordinator. Also look to diocesan and other national newspapers and journals.

America Magazine. "The Word" department. Weekly.

> Commentary on the Sunday Lectionary texts.

The Sunday website at Saint Louis University, The Center for Liturgy at Saint Louis University. www.liturgy.slu.edu.

> Several authors address: praying toward Sunday, spirituality for Sunday, get to know the readings, music. English and Spanish.

Jay Cormier, ed. *Connections: Ideas, Resources, and Information for Homilist and Preachers.* Monthly. Connections/Media Works, 7 Lantern Lane, Londonderry, NH 03053-3905. (603) 432-6056. Web: www.connections mediaworks.com.

> Exegesis and notes on the gospel; other connections for daily life; special issues.

Xavier Leon-Dufour. *Dictionary of Biblical Theology.* New York: Seabury Press, 1973. Paper, 1995.

Daniel J. Harrington, SJ, ed. Sacra Pagina series. Collegeville, MN: Liturgical Press.

> A commentary on the books of the New Testament. Several volumes.

Homily Helps for Sundays. Cincinnati: Franciscan Media, monthly. info .FranciscanMedia.org.

John Kavanaugh, SJ. *The Word Embodied (Year A). The Word Encountered (Year B). The Word Engaged (Year C).* Maryknoll, NY: Orbis Books.

> Three volumes of meditations on the Sunday Scriptures.

5. Some BIBLE COMMENTARIES:

Dianne Bergant and Robert Karris, gen. eds. *The Collegeville Bible Commentary.* Collegeville, MN: Liturgical Press, 1992.

Raymond E. Brown, SS, Joseph A. Fitzmyer, SJ, Roland E. Murphy, OCarm, eds. *The New Jerome Biblical Commentary.* Englewood Cliffs, NJ: Prentice Hall, 1990. Revised edition, 1999.

The Anchor Bible commentary series. New York: Doubleday.
>   Individual volume(s) for each book of the Bible.

6. Some invaluable works on METHOD AND WAYS of hearing Scripture:

National Conference of Catholic Bishops, Committee on Priestly Life and Ministry. *Fulfilled in Your Hearing: The Homily in the Sunday Assembly.* Washington, DC: United States Catholic Conference, 1992.
>   Also found in *The Liturgy Documents, Volume One*. Fifth edition. Chicago: Liturgy Training Publications.

Congregation for Divine Worship and the Discipline of the Sacraments. *Homiletic Directory*. Washington, DC: USCCB, 2014.
>   Part I treats the homily and its liturgical setting; part II covers essential questions of method and content for the seasons. Appendix I cites the CCC for the Sunday biblical texts; appendix II cites key postconciliar sources for preaching.

James B. Dunning. *Echoing God's Word: Formation for Catechists and Homilists in a Catechumenal Church.* Arlington, VA: The North American Forum on the Catechumenate, 1993.

6. REDRAFTING *the focus*

1. What adjustments are needed on the chosen focus because of the exegesis?

2. What best meets the needs of the church and the catechumenal community?

7. DESIGNING *the week*

1. How will this week's TRAINING AND FORMATION IN THE CHRISTIAN LIFE foster the pastoral needs detailed in the *Rite of Christian Initiation of Adults*, 75:
   a) Suitable catechesis accommodated to the liturgical year
   b) Familiarity with the communal Christian way of life
   c) Suitable liturgical rites

d) The apostolic life or life of Christian witness

What prayer(s) from the Rites Belonging to the Period of the Catechumenate (RCIA 81–103) are suitable? What else may be suitable?

2. Works to consult on ADULT METHODS FOR CHRISTIAN FORMATION:

Thomas Groome. *Sharing Faith: A Comprehensive Approach to Religious
Education and Pastoral Ministry.* New York: HarperSanFrancisco, 1991.

An invaluable work on a METHOD for doing catechesis and preaching; describes the shared Christian praxis method. After a focusing
activity, it has five movements:

a) Naming/Expressing "Present Praxis"

b) Critical Reflection on Present Action

c) Making Accessible Christian Story and Vision

d) Dialectical Hermeneutic to Appropriate Christian Story and Vision

e) Decision/Response for Lived Christian Faith

Michael Clay. *A Harvest for God: Christian Initiation in the Rural and Small-
Town Parish.* Chicago: Liturgy Training Publications, 2003.

Chapter 4 on the period of the catechumenate treats catechesis for this
period, the importance of dismissal, how to prepare and facilitate
catechetical sessions, and use of the Rites Belonging to the Period of
the Catechumenate. Appendix 4 provides a list of suitable topics on
church teachings that emerge from the liturgical year. Appendixes 5–8
are also helpful.

Gilbert Ostdiek. *Catechesis for Liturgy: A Program for Parish Involvement.*
Portland, OR: OCP, 1986.

Chapter 1 nicely summarizes three models for Christian formation:
mystagogical catechesis, Groome's shared Christian praxis, and the
author's method used in the book:

a) Attending to what we and others actually experience

b) Reflecting on what our experience and that of others means

c) Applying what we have learned to future celebrations

Joe Paprocki. *Beyond the Catechist's Toolbox: Catechesis That Not Only Informs but Also Transforms.* Chicago: Loyola Press, 2013.

Stresses the need to know the language of mystery to do catechesis.
Provides a five-stage catechetical process: Preliminaries, Engage, Explore, Reflect, and Respond.

3. Some works to consult for BRIEF COMMENTARY and RE-
   FLECTION QUESTIONS:

At Home with the Word: Sunday Scriptures and Reflections. Chicago: Liturgy
Training Publications, annual.

> Contains NABRE text with reflection questions and Christian practice
> suggestions.

Workbook for Lectors and Gospel Readers and/or: *Manual para proclamadores
de la palabra.* Chicago: Liturgy Training Publications, annuals.

> Separate editions for the United States in English (NABRE) and Span-
> ish and for Canada (NRSV); prints all four texts; brief commentary;
> tips for good proclamation.

*Living Liturgy: Spirituality, Celebration, and Catechesis for Sundays and
Solemnities.* Collegeville, MN: Liturgical Press, annual.

> Contains primary Sunday and solemnity texts (collect and readings),
> gospel reflections, connections between the readings, faith-sharing
> questions, support for ministers, homily points, and so on.

*Sourcebook for Sundays, Seasons, and Weekdays: The Almanac for Pastoral
Liturgy.* Chicago: Liturgy Training Publications, annual.

> Contains overviews for the primary ritual books; then for each season
> treats the meaning, the texts and the liturgies and the ministers, and
> the calendar. Note the special attention given to the *Rite of Christian
> Initiation of Adults.*

Give Us This Day: Daily Prayer for Today's Catholic. Collegeville, MN: Liturgical Press, twelve issues annually.

> Contains Mass readings, prayers, and reflection for each day plus a
> simple setting for Morning and Evening Prayer, the Order of Mass,
> brief articles, suitable songs, and religious art.

*Living the Word: Scripture Reflections and Commentaries for Sundays and
Holy Days.* Franklin Park, IL: World Library Publications, annual.

> Contains NABRE text used in the US Lectionary; understanding the
> word; reflecting on the word; responding to the word.

Joan Mitchell, ed. *Sunday by Sunday: Lectionary-based Reflection for Adults.*
St. Paul: Good Ground Press, seven units annually. (800) 232-5533.

> Four pages each week to help adults to reflect on the readings; ques-
> tions can be helpful in session design.

The Word Among Us. Frederick, MD: The Word Among Us Press, twelve issues annually. (800) 775-9673. www.wau.org.

> Daily meditations on one of the assigned readings. Version with Mass Readings Supplement also provides the texts for the Mass antiphons, prayers, as well as readings.

4. Some works to consult for commentary, reflection questions, and SESSION OUTLINES AND SUGGESTIONS:

Leisa Anslinger, Mary A. Ehle, Biagio Mazza, Victoria M. Tufano. *The Living Word: Leading RCIA Dismissals*. Chicago: Liturgy Training Publications, Year B, 2017; Year C, 2018; Year A, 2019.

> Provides background for dismissal from the Liturgy of the Word and the praying that follows. For each Sunday, offers suggestions to reflect on the experience. It also lists possible topics for extended catechesis. Perhaps too much information for dismissal prayer; usable for extended catechesis.

Kathy Brown, Bob Duggan, Carol Gura, Rita Ferrone, Gael Gensler, Maureen Kelly, Steve Lanza, Donna Steffen. *Foundations in Faith: Catechist Manual Catechumenate*. Three volumes. Allen: Resources for Christian Living, Year A, 1998; Year B, 1999; Year C, 1997. (800) 527-5030.

> Provides background for catechesis on the Scripture, Catholic doctrine, and Catholic culture; session plans for dismissal and extended catechesis.

Gael Gensler, OSF, and Rev. Steven Lanza. *Apprentices in Faith*. www.apprenticesinfaith.com. (877) 275-4725. By mail: RCL Benziger, 8805 Governor's Hill Dr., Suite 400, Cincinnati, OH 45249. Annual subscription.

> Online resources of all three Lectionary years for the baptismal catechumenate. Samples and scope of offerings posted on web.

Margaret Nutting Ralph. *Breaking Open the Lectionary: Lectionary Readings in Their Biblical Context for RCIA, Faith Sharing Groups, and Lectors*. New York: Paulist Press, *Cycle B*, 2005; *Cycle C*, 2006; *Cycle A*, 2007.

> Provides three- to four-page commentary on the Scripture and questions for various groups.

Mary Birmingham. *Word and Worship Workbook: For Ministry in Initiation for Year A, Preaching, Religious Education and Formation*. Mahwah, NJ: Paulist Press, 1999; *Year B*, 2000; *Year C*, 1998.

Provides suggestions for environment and prayer; extensive commentary on the texts; a five-step process for catechesis.

Celebrating the Lectionary. Chicago: Liturgy Training Publications, annual.

Intergenerational catechetical material from nursery through youth; based on the *Lectionary for Mass*.

Maureen Kelly. *Children's Liturgy of the Word: A Weekly Resource*. Chicago: Liturgy Training Publications, annual.

This annual covers September through August, spanning two liturgical years treating Sundays and solemnities. Contains a helpful introduction on the prayer leader's role, celebrating the Liturgy of the Word with children, and a most helpful chart of dates, themes, and readings. For each season, there is an introduction; then Scripture background, preparation, and liturgy guide for each celebration.

Living the Good News. New York: Church Publishing Inc./Morehouse Educational Resources, online. www.livingthegoodnews.com.

Intergenerational catechetical material from pre-school through adult; based on the *Lectionary for Mass*; separate booklet on Liturgy of the Word with children. Use the Roman Catholic edition.

Jerry Galipeau. *Apprenticed to Christ: Activities for Practicing the Catholic Way of Life*. Franklin Park, IL: World Library Publications, 2007.

In a half-page for each Sunday of liturgical years A, B, and C, the author cites a text from one of the readings, gives an apprenticeship activity, provides one or more Christian formation topics, and lists catechetical resources. A gem, "A Catechetical Method: Mystagogical Catechesis in the Session for Christian Formation," is on page 8.

Jerry Galipeau. *We Send You Forth: Dismissals for the RCIA*. Franklin Park, IL: World Library Publications, 2005.

These dismissals use ritual language to connect the biblical themes and images of each Sunday or solemnity to what catechumens will ponder. Clip art by Br. Michael McGrath. CD-ROM allows reprinting of a given text.

5. Some resources to consult for MUSIC:

World Library Publications. *AIM Liturgy Magazine*. WLP, 3708 River Road, Suite 400, Franklin Park, IL 60131-2158. (800) 566-6150. www .wlpmusic.com.

GIA Publications, Inc. *GIA Quarterly: A Liturgical Music Journal*. GIA, 7404 S. Mason Ave., Chicago, IL 60638. (800) 422-1358. www.giamusic.com.

Oregon Catholic Press. *Liturgia y Canción* and *Today's Liturgy*. OCP, 5536 NE Hassalo, Portland, OR 97213-3638. (800) 548-8749. www.ocp.org.

8. SHARING the design

1. With whom is this design shared? Preacher, presiding minister, dismissal minister, catechumenate period coordinator, and so on.

2. What handouts need to be prepared? Are copyright permissions needed?